Glorious Roots

LAURENCE SOMBKE

GLORIOUS ROOTS

Recipes for Healthy, Tasty Vegetables

MASTERMEDIA LIMITED

NEW YORK

Library of Congress Cataloging-in-Publication Data
Sombke, Laurence.
  Glorious roots : recipes for healthy, tasty vegetables / Laurence Sombke.
  p.   cm.
  Includes index.
  ISBN 0-942361-33-4 (hardcover)
  1. Cookery (Vegetables) 1. Root-crops. I. Title.
TX801.S62 1992
641.6'51—dc20   91-60809
                                                           CIP

Production services by Martin Cook Associates, Ltd.
Designed by Jacqueline Schuman
Manufactured in the United States of America

*I want to dedicate this book
to my wife, Catherine Herman, and our
two children, Henry and Kit, because
they make my life so wonderful.*

Contents

Glorious Roots

Introduction: The Roots Renaissance

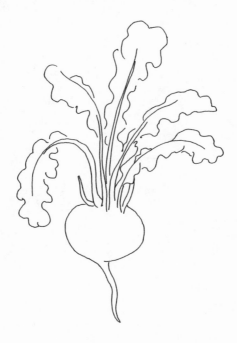

The Roots Legacy

People have been eating roots ever since they learned they could simply bend over and pull them up from the ground. Along with berries and wild game, roots were always on the menu at the primitive family's dinner table.

Roots have been an important food source for people around the world for hundreds, even thousands, of years. Europeans have eaten parsnips, turnips, and onions since Roman times and before. Pre-Columbian Americans ate potatoes long before they were "discovered" by the conquistadors. Africans have depended on cassava and yam since the earliest days of civilization. Asians have made daikon radishes, ginger, and other roots a necessary part of their culinary palette.

Roots fell into disfavor in the 1960s with the style-setting leaders of American food trends. Restaurants forgot that roots even existed, except as an afterthought. As produce growers in California, Texas, Florida, and elsewhere improved their techniques, succulent glamour vegetables like broccoli, artichokes, asparagus, lettuce, tomatoes, and cucumbers began to take over the main parts of the produce aisle at supermarkets. Except for carrots and potatoes, roots, like turnips, parsnips, and beets, became more and more obscure.

The Roots Revolution

The 1990s have begun with a roots renaissance. What was old is now new again. Chefs are dressing them up and giving them high profile in tony restaurants. New colorful and exotic varieties are showing up in the produce aisle. We are discovering what people have known for centuries—roots are tasty, economical, and probably, above all, healthy.

ROOTS ARE HEALTHY

One of the most important reasons that roots are making a comeback is that they are so healthy to eat. Roots are extremely low in calories and salt. They contain no fat or cholesterol except for the cream sauce you put on top. They are very good sources of complex carbohydrates, dietary fiber, vitamins A and C, as well as the minerals potassium and iron.

Naturally, the best way to improve your health through food is to eat a balanced diet that includes fresh fruits and vegetables, meats, beans, fish, dairy products, and whole grains. You should also stop smoking and start exercising.

Eating more root vegetables is a very good way to increase your intake of fresh fruits and vegetables. Eating roots can:

Help you lose weight. Since roots, like most other fresh fruits and vegetables, are 80 to 95 percent water, they are very low in calories. A cup of cooked carrots contains only 48 calories, an average potato about 110 calories.

Most weight-reducing plans let you eat an unlimited amount of fresh vegetables. Many business people who used to have bowls of candy on their desks to snack on and offer visitors now place bags of cut carrots within easy reach. Radishes and turnip slices are also excellent low-calorie snack foods.

Roots, especially potatoes, are very good complex carbohydrates. We used to think that eating too many starchy foods such as potatoes would cause you to gain weight. Now, we have found that eating complex carbohydrates such as root vegetables is better for you than eating high-fat foods such as meat.

Furthermore, complex carbohydrates release their food energy to your body more slowly and over a long period of time. This means that you will feel more energetic and less bloated.

Help prevent heart disease. One of the most important factors leading to heart disease is a diet too high in fat, especially saturated fat, which tends to be high in cholesterol. A high-fat diet can elevate your cholesterol and cause you to gain weight. You can lower your cholesterol by eliminating high-fat snack food like cakes and cookies and reducing your portions of meat and dairy products. But you say you're still hungry? Fill that void by eating root vegetables.

Help prevent cancer. Eating root vegetables can help prevent cancer in two ways:

1. Beta carotene. Beta carotene is the chemical found in many foods that transforms into vitamin A once it is in your body. Numerous studies by research labs, doctors, and hospitals now indicate that people who eat foods with an adequate supply of vitamin A can reduce their risk of lung, breast, and intestinal cancers.

Carrots, sweet potatoes, rutabaga, beet greens, and turnip greens are outstanding sources of dietary vitamin A. One carrot or one average-size sweet potato will provide more than the minimum daily requirement of vitamin A.

2. Crucifers. Cruciferous vegetables are all the vegetables that are members of the cabbage family. Again, scientific studies are beginning to point to substances in cruciferous vegetables as a key element in preventing the growth and spread of cancer of the stomach, colon, and large intestine.

Turnips are not members of the cabbage family, but turnip greens contain the same cancer-blocking qualities as cabbage.

Help lower your cholesterol. Eating a diet high in dietary fiber can help lower your cholesterol level. Dietary fiber helps block the body's absorption or retention of cholesterol. It helps carry excess cholesterol out of the body. Roots are very high in dietary fiber.

Help improve your digestion and body functions. If you treat your body to a diet that is full of fiber-rich root vegetables, it has an easier time digesting that food and passing it through the body. You can become more regular and have less indigestion.

Also, roots . . .

Are a good source of vitamins and minerals. In addition to beta carotene/vitamin A and the other cancer-fighting substances, root vegetables are a good source of vitamins and minerals.

One-half cup of raw turnips or rutabaga contains a whole day's supply of vitamin C. Potatoes, sweet potatoes, beets, and carrots are also good sources of vitamin C.

Turnips, parsnips, and celery root are very good sources of potassium.

ROOTS ARE HIP

Chefs, restaurateurs, and food writers are constantly on the lookout for new food trends and new foods to keep the public coming back for more. Luckily, root vegetables are back in style after the nouvelle cuisine and relentless restaurant mania of the 1980s. Cooks are looking for healthier foods that are bright and colorful yet display a true depth of flavor. Roots fit the bill on all counts. Why are roots so popular?

Comfort food. After the onslaught of assertive and sometimes challenging food trends of Szechuan, Cajun/Creole, Thai, Mexican, and others, people started yearning for the foods their mothers used to make. They wanted mashed potatoes, vegetable soup, pot roast, and anything else that was soothing, familiar, and, well, comfortable. Roots are old-fashioned, peasant, vintage, heirloom foods that Grandmother used to mash and butter and pile on your plate for Sunday dinner. Mashed potatoes became a rage and were served at fancy restaurants with $4 price tags.

Bistro food. Bistro food is comfort food based on the cozy corner restaurants of Paris and other cities in France. Traditional bistro meals are steak and French fries, casseroles, mashed potatoes, skillet-braised turnips, and buttered carrots Vichy. Bistro food features a variety of root vegetables, especially that famous French charcuterie special céleri rémoulade—celery root salad in a tart mayonnaise.

Haute cuisine. Not to be outdone, the top chefs at the best restaurants in America began to feature roots on their menus. The Union

Square Café in New York serves a vegetable plate that might carry purées of turnips and potatoes flavored with cheeses and other garnishes. Oprah Winfrey's Eccentric in Chicago has a signature dish that is nothing more than lumpy mashed potatoes spiked with horseradish. Deep-fried celeriac and sweet potatoes, poached fish on a bed of mashed potatoes, and beets in salads seem to be everywhere.

Caribbean and international. Foods from the islands of Jamaica, Puerto Rico, Barbados, Trinidad, Martinique, and other parts of the West Indies seem to be increasingly available throughout the United States. As more and more people from the West Indies migrate to the United States, and as more and more Americans travel south for vacations, foods from that part of the world are getting better known. Boniato, cassava, malanga, taro, and yam are common everyday root vegetables there, and they are beginning to show up in restaurants and produce aisles here.

Foods from Mexico and the Far East are also getting a lot of play recently. Crunch jicama is very common south of the border, while daikon radish, ginger, and turnips are used often in Thai, Chinese, Korean, and Japanese cooking.

ROOTS ARE ECONOMICAL AND AVAILABLE YEAR-ROUND

Long before the advent of fancy foods like kiwi, avocado, and snow peas in winter, people depended on reliable roots to feed them year-round, from season to season. Roots are easy to grow, they don't get killed by frosts like oranges, they can be stored for months in a cool, dry area, and they are always reasonably priced. Other virtues:

Economical. The more common a root vegetable is, the cheaper it is to buy. Carrots, potatoes, onions, turnips, rutabaga, and sweet potatoes rarely ever get above 35 to 50 cents per pound. Potatoes can be as little as 10 cents a pound. Some of the more exotic roots such as parsnips, celeriac, jicama, daikon, and fresh beets can be a little more expensive. But even the Caribbean roots like cassava and malanga rarely get above $1 a pound.

Not perishable and very little waste. Once you buy root vegetables, they will store for 2 weeks or so in a cool, dry place or in a refrigerator at your home. There is no fat, bone, gristle, scales, heels, cardboard boxes, fancy packaging, or other waste associated with roots. Most of the time you simply peel them, cook them, and eat them.

New varieties. Blue, purple, yellow, and pink potatoes, golden beets, boutique onions, manioc, Hamburg parsley, black radishes, radish sprouts, and other types of exotic root vegetables are appearing in the fresh produce aisle right along with tamarind, multicolored egg roll wrappers, fresh herbs, and kim chee.

New produce varieties help bring color and excitement to shoppers and cooks who are looking for a break from the usual routine of family dinners. Three companies are chiefly responsible for bringing new root varieties to supermarkets. Contact any of them for more information about tropical fruits and vegetables as well as other unusual foods.

1. Freida's Finest, P.O. Box 58488, Los Angeles, CA 90058, 213-627-2981. Freida Caplan introduced kiwi to the United States and she has brought us many new fruits and vegetables since then.

2. J. R. Brooks & Son, Inc., P.O. Drawer 9, Homestead, FL 33090, 800-327-4833. Dade County, Florida, is a major producer of tropical Caribbean root vegetables in the United States, largely because of the huge Cuban population there but also because of the climate. Brooks is a major grower, packer, and shipper of tropical roots as well as tropical fruits such as papaya, carambola, and mango.

3. Melissa's Brand, World Variety Produce, P.O. Box 21127, Los Angeles, CA 90021, 213-588-0151. Melissa's is a relative newcomer to the world of exotic produce, but they supply supermarkets with a complete selection of Caribbean root vegetables as well as other fruits and vegetables from around the world.

A Root-by-Root Look at Roots

A more exact subtitle for this book would be *Most of the Vegetables That Grow Underground.* That's because some of the vegetables included are not true roots. Potatoes are tubers, onions are bulbs, and ginger is a rhizome. But for the purposes of people's perception of what is and isn't a root, and for the purposes of great-tasting meals, they have been included.

In addition, there are several foods that grow underground that are not included. Peanuts grow underground, but in people's perception they are nuts, not root vegetables. Kudzu and lotus root, while popular in Asia, are rarely available here in their fresh form.

Finally, there are new roots being rediscovered, grown, tested, and imported all the time. Many of the roots on the following list were not well known or easy to purchase or grow just five years ago. Several previously unknown roots will be on the market by the time this book is published. But that's fine. Any new roots that can raise awareness about the root's nutrition and flavor are welcome.

BEETS

Unfortunately, beets are one vegetable that too many people think come pickled in a jar. Pickled beets are wonderful, but they are not the end-all of beet cookery. The sweet flavor of beets is delicious in both hot and cold borscht, or steamed and sliced and tossed with herbs or grated into a salad and dressed with vinaigrette.

How to buy. Choose medium-sized beets with a deep red color and smooth skin. A wrinkled beet is an old beet. Try to buy beets that still have their tops attached. Fresh-looking greens are a sign that the flesh is fresh, too.

The best season for beets is from June through November, but they are often available in other months. They are usually sold three or four to a bunch for prices generally under $1.

Red beets are by far the most common, but watch for long, thin beets called cylindra that are perfect for slicing, golden beets that are round and yellow and don't bleed when cooked, and the candy-striped Italian Chioggia beets that have white streaks mixed in with the red.

How to handle. Remove the beet greens and eat them within a day or two, while they are still fresh and crisp. Trim the stems to within 1 inch of the beet and wash them. You can store fresh beets in the refrigerator for up to 10 days, but it is best if you eat them right away.

To prevent beets from bleeding when you cook them, follow these simple tips:

1. Trim the stems to within 1 inch from the top.
2. Don't peel the beets before cooking.
3. Leave the root tips intact.
4. Wash and put them in water to cover.
5. Peel and slice beets after they are cooked.
6. Add beets to other ingredients right before serving.

Nutritional value. One-half cup cooked beets has 30 calories, 43 grams of sodium, plus dietary fiber and smaller amounts of vitamin C, iron, and potassium.

History and folklore. Beets are native to Europe and North Africa. The Romans ate beets, although they were longer and thinner than the globe-shaped beets we eat today. It wasn't until the 1700s that today's beets began to be grown in Europe and America.

How to grow your own. Beets will grow in any crumbly, well-drained soil over a wide variety of climates. Plant in the early spring for a summer harvest or in the late summer for a fall harvest. Beets mature in about 50 to 60 days from the time they are planted.

BEET GREENS

Beet greens are the leaves of the rooted beet plant. They are dark green and crinkly and tinged with red. They are delicious when they are fresh and tender simply added to a lettuce salad and tossed with vinaigrette dressing. Or steam beet greens and serve wilted with a hot bacon vinaigrette. Beet greens also can be chopped and added to stir-fried pork or beef or tossed into minestrone soup.

Beet greens are a very good source of vitamin A. One-half cup of cooked beet greens provides a day's supply of vitamin A.

CARROTS

Carrots are everybody's favorite root vegetable. They are so common and well liked that it is easy to forget that they actually grow underground and that they are very rich in vitamin A.

How to buy. Carrots can be either long and thin or short and stubby. Choose carrots that are bright colored, smooth skinned, and fresh looking. Carrots with tops are the freshest because tops will wither and dry out quickly. Packaged carrots are still very high quality if they have been handled and stored well.

Carrots are available year-round, but try buying some from a local farmers' market to get a good old-fashioned taste of carrots fresh from the ground.

How to handle. Carrots will store well for a month in your home refrigerator, but eventually they will start to dry and wither. According to Cornell University research, the vitamins in carrots are spread throughout the flesh and are not concentrated near the skin as some people previously thought. This means that you can peel carrots and still retain all of their vitamins. Carrots are perfectly good to eat if they are simply scrubbed with cold water, but go ahead and peel them if you want to.

Nutritional value. Carrots are a very good source of vitamin A. A single average-sized carrot contains the full daily requirement of vitamin A. It has only 20 calories and 24 grams of sodium.

History and folklore. Carrots originated in India, Afghanistan, and eastern Russia, and then migrated to Europe, China, and the rest of the world. Carrot seeds dating from 3000 to 2000 B.C. have been found in ancient caves in Switzerland.

The earliest uses for carrots were medicinal. Carrots weren't eaten for food until the twelfth century. Italians began eating them in the thirteenth century, and the Dutch, Germans, and English began eating them in the fourteenth and fifteenth centuries.

Carrots are members of the parsley family, which also includes dill, fennel, caraway, and 2,500 other plants. Carrots also are related to a wild weed called Queen Anne's lace, a feathery green plant with a white lacy flower that is very common along the American roadside in summer.

How to grow your own. Carrots are relatively easy to grow as long as the soil is dug up to a depth of 10 inches and is really free of rocks and stones. Many gardeners prefer to grow carrots in raised beds that have been mixed with a lot of sand and compost.

Carrot types can be as long as the 8-inch Imperator or as short as the 2-inch baby carrots. All have great flavor.

Carrots are ready to eat 65 to 75 days after they are planted. Plant them in the early spring for a summer harvest or in the late summer for a fall crop.

CELERY ROOT

Celery root is little known to Americans except for an infrequent appearance in gourmet produce stores. But in France, céleri is exalted in the ubiquitous charcuterie salad céleri-rave rémoulade, or grated celery root with herb mayonnaise. It is also very well known in Germany, where it is creamed and served as a side dish. Recently, though, the céleri chip, deep-fried celeriac, has become the darling of bistro chefs across the U.S.A.

How to buy. Celery root, also called celeriac and knob celery, is, genetically speaking, the sibling of the tall stalk celery we all know and love. Even though celery and celery root have a similar flavor, visually they are worlds apart. Celery is graceful, long and green. Celery root is a dusty-white bulbous root.

Choose roots that are about 3 to 4 inches in diameter, about the size of a large apple, and have smooth, uncracked skin. You are most likely to find celeriac in grocery stores from September through March, but watch for it in November and December at farmers' markets. Because it is not yet commonly available, celery root can be priced at $1 to $1.50 per pound.

How to handle. Celery root in a plastic bag in the refrigerator will keep from 10 days to 2 weeks.

To cook, wash and peel the root and slice it. The skin of celery root can be difficult to peel. Use a sharp paring knife and peel it like an apple instead of like a carrot. If you plan to use it as crudité or hold it for deep frying, it is best to place the celery root in water that has had lemon slices or lemon juice added to prevent discoloring.

Nutritional value. Celery root is a good source of potassium and dietary fiber, but it offers little else in the way of vitamins and minerals. It is low in calories.

History and folklore. Celery root is related to stalk celery and is a member of the parsley family. It probably originated in the areas around the Mediterranean Sea and then spread to other parts of Europe.

How to grow your own. Celery root is difficult to grow because it takes a hot growing season at least 120 days long. It is also slow to germinate. Start the seeds indoors and transplant as soon as the ground can be worked. They prefer a sunny, ordinary soil free of rocks.

JICAMA

One of the great benefits of the spread of more authentic Mexican foods in recent years has been the discovery of jicama, a crunchy vegetable popular south of the border that is replacing fried tortilla chips for low-calorie salsa dipping.

How to buy. Jicama has a crispy white flesh that is similar in texture to turnips and radishes, but its flavor is mild and bland, not spicy or bitter. It has a very thin beige-colored skin. Generally, it is a round root with a narrow neck and a lobed body.

Choose jicama that weighs from ½ pound to 1 pound, approximately the size of a large orange. Many jicama are larger than that, but they run the risk of being woody and tough.

How to handle. Jicama can be eaten raw or cooked. Simply peel off the outer skin and a thin layer of fibrous white flesh underneath. Then you can slice, grate, or chop it to your specifications. In Mexico, it is often sliced thin and eaten with salsa or just munched, sprinkled with a dusting of lime and chili powder. In Asian cooking, jicama is added to stir-fries, where its taste and texture are good substitutes for water chestnuts.

Nutritional value. Jicama is very low in calories and sodium and is a good source of fiber.

History and folklore. The English name for jicama is yam bean because it not only produces the edible root but also a poisonous pod on its vines, which grow above the ground. The Chinese name is saa got. Jicama is native to Mexico and South America but has been eaten in Asia since it was introduced to the Philippines by the Spanish in the seventeenth century.

How to grow your own. Unless you live in South Texas or in a similar climate, it is probably better to buy jicama at the grocery store because it requires a very long and hot growing season.

ONIONS, GARLIC, LEEKS, SCALLIONS, AND SHALLOTS

Welcome to the wonderful world of onions. First of all, it is important to note that onions, garlic, and shallots are not roots. They are bulbs and members of the lily family Allium. But they are included in this book because they are a wonderful food source that grows underground, they are inexpensive, they store a long time, and they add fiber and flavor, not fat, to foods.

Most people are aware of the familiar red, yellow, and white dry onions, but there are also fresh onions that look like dry ones but actually should be eaten right away. Then there are shallots, leeks, scallions, and even garlic which are all members of the onion family. This section is going to introduce you to the wide variety of onions, how to identify, buy, store, and use them.

Dry Onions

These familiar onions, also called globe onions because of their shape, are grown for their ability to store well over winter. They can certainly be eaten when they first come onto the market in October and November, but they are equally good to eat in March and April. Common types are the mild-tasting and light-golden Bermuda, the large, tangy red Spanish, the pungent yellow and white, which are both better cooked.

Choose dry onions that are clean and firm without any bruises or cracks. Avoid ones that are spongy or beginning to sprout. They will keep for 3 to 4 weeks if stored in a dry room-temperature spot.

Fresh Onions

Fresh onions are the new glamour onions coming on the market with names such as Vidalia, Texas SpringSweet, California Sweet Imperials, Walla Walla Sweets, and Mauis. These are the onions that top chefs are using in their special dishes, placing their names on the menu.

Whereas the dry onions are generally better cooked, these fresh onions are so sweet they are delicious raw on sandwiches and in salads. They have lighter color and thinner skins, and they are more susceptible to bruising and decay. It is better to refrigerate these onions and use them within a week to 10 days.

Leeks and Scallions

Leeks are most often cooked and rarely eaten raw. Look for tender leeks that are medium to small and have a good 2 to 3 inches of white stem before the green stalk begins. Wash leeks very well to remove any embedded grit before cooking them. They will store wrapped in the refrigerator for 3 to 5 days.

Scallions are also known as spring, salad, or bunching onions. They easily find their way raw onto salad platters and are tasty cooked in stir-fries and scrambled eggs. They will store well 2 to 4 days wrapped in the refrigerator.

Shallots and Garlic

These two tiny gourmet onions are packed with flavor. A little bit goes a long way. Garlic grows as the tightly packaged bulb we see in the market, but shallots grow as an unruly clump that is separated into individual cloves. They are sold bagged or loose. They most resemble oversized garlic cloves wrapped in a red or brown skin.

Peel a shallot as you would an ordinary dry or fresh onion. Peel a garlic by laying a clove on a wooden cutting board. Hold your knife over it with the flat side resting on top of the garlic clove. Smash the other flat side of the knife with your hand and the skin will pop off the garlic clove. Then chop the garlic and add it to your dish.

Nutritional value. Onions are very low in calories and do contain some vitamin C. A typical medium onion weighing 150 grams (a little more than ½ cup) contains about 60 calories. A cup of cooked onions contains one-third the adult recommended daily supply of vitamin C.

History and folklore. All types of onions are considered to be native to central Asia, northwestern India, and Afghanistan. They have been eaten and cultivated by people since the dawn of history. The workers who built the pyramids of Egypt were fed huge quantities of onions, garlic, and radishes. Onions were brought to the New World by the Spanish and cultivation has spread since then.

How to grow yourself. Dry onions will grow almost anywhere in the world as long as the soil is rich and well drained. Most people plant onion sets in early spring as soon as the ground can be worked, and then harvest in the fall. Plant individual shallot cloves in the early spring for a fall harvest of a clump. Scallions, garlic, and leeks are better planted in the fall, covered for winter protection, and harvested the next year. Nurseries and catalogues carry an enormous variety and selection of all types of onions.

PARSLEY ROOT

Parsley root is a variety of parsley except that it is grown for its long white root rather than its green leafy top. It is also commonly called Hamburg parsley because it is much admired and savored in German-speaking countries. It has a mild, earthy flavor and the lovely aroma of fresh parsley. The flat green leaves are good to eat, too.

How to buy. Parsley root resembles parsnips in color, shape, and texture. You can tell them apart by the leafy green parsley tops that not only look like parsley but smell like it, too. Look for roots that are creamy colored, firm, and free of blemishes. They aren't always easy to find at the market, but they are available. Ask your greengrocer to get some for you. They will last up to a week wrapped and kept in the refrigerator.

How to handle. Wash the roots and stems. Cut the stems from the roots and place them in a plastic bag, to be used chopped like regular parsley. Peel the roots if you like, but they aren't bitter. The roots are good cooked and added to soups and stews and mashed into purées with potatoes or other roots.

Nutritional value. Parsley root is high in fiber and a good source of vitamin C.

History and folklore. Not much is known about parsley root apart from regular parsley, which was prized by the Greeks as a decorative herb but widely eaten as food by the Romans.

How to garden. Parsley root will grow in any rich, well-tilled soil. Plant it as you would carrots and beets, keep the area weeded, and harvest in the fall.

PARSNIPS

How to buy. A well-grown parsnip will be a light creamy-beige color, about 6 to 8 inches long, 1 inch wide at the crown and tapering toward the bottom. Most of the time they are bunched in a plastic bag at the market, but be sure to look inside for roots that are firm, clean, unblemished, and straight—not forked. Parsnips can be woody, especially at the core, but not if they are fresh and perfectly sized.

How to handle. Wash and trim the parsnip, and peel it if you like. Slice it into chunks for soups and stews or into chips for French fries. Leave them whole for pot roast. But if you slice them lengthwise and sauté them in butter, they become soft and have a sweet, nutty flavor.

Nutritional value. One cup of cooked parsnips contains only 66 calories and 8 milligrams of sodium, but adds a goodly 375 milligrams of potassium.

History and folklore. Parsnips are native to the eastern Mediterranean and northward into Russia. The ancient Romans ate parsnips and the emperor Tiberius had them brought to him from Germany, then part of ancient Gaul, because they were especially good from that region.

Parsnips were a main staple in the diet of the Middle Ages, before the potato was discovered in the New World and brought to Europe. Parsnips were grown extensively in the American colonies and were quite popular with American Indians, who also cultivated them.

How to grow. Parsnips grow just like carrots and parsley root. Be sure the soil is deeply dug and free of stones. Plant in the spring and harvest in the fall. If winter is mild in your area, cover your parsnips with mulch and dig them up over the course of the winter. Cool weather helps turn their starch to sugar and makes them sweeter to eat.

POTATOES

Of course, potatoes are not really roots, either. They are tubers that grow underground. But since they are so widely used in much the same way as many roots and they often appear along with roots in so many dishes, it is important to include them here.

The fortunes of potatoes as a nutritious food to eat have taken a positive upturn in the last few years. People used to think that starchy potatoes were fattening. But now people see potatoes as a miracle food because that starch turns out to be an excellent source of complex carbohydrates. Nutritionists are now encouraging us to eat potatoes because they are low in fat and sodium and high in complex carbohydrates, the kind that slowly changes to sugar in our bodies, giving us extra energy all day long.

Keeping up with the nutritional turnaround for potatoes is the increasing variety of potatoes now coming onto the market. In addition to fluffy russet potatoes, waxy red potatoes, and all-purpose Kennebec potatoes, we are now seeing purple, gold-yellow, and pink potatoes. Restaurant chefs and home cooks who are always looking for something flavorful and colorful have latched on to these new spuds and given potatoes an elevated position on their plates of food. Here's a sampling of the potato picks.

Russet Burbank. This is the long, brown-skinned baking potato that is often called an Idaho potato, although it is also grown commercially in Washington, Oregon, and Prince Edward Island, Canada. Its texture is fluffy, light, and a little mealy, and it is best suited for baking, French-frying, and microwaving.

Kennebec. This is the round "Irish cobbler" potato with smooth white skin and white flesh. It is an all-purpose potato that is good for baking, boiling, or frying. It is grown commercially in Maine, Upstate New York and Long Island, Wisconsin, and Prince Edward Island.

Red Pontiac or Chieftain. This is the medium-sized red potato with white waxy skin. It is delicious boiled and served with butter, and it is the perfect potato for potato salad.

Yukon Gold. This is a fairly new potato on the market. It is medium size with yellow-brown skin and yellow flesh. This is an all-purpose potato that does seem to have a buttery flavor, giving you the opportunity to use a little less butter when you serve it.

What are new potatoes? New potatoes are not a special type of potato. They are simply potatoes that are freshly dug. They are oftentimes smaller than older potatoes because farmers and consumers just can't wait for them to be fully mature before they dig up and eat the first potatoes of the new season.

How to buy. Choose potatoes that are clean looking, smooth skinned, firm, and heavy to the touch. Avoid potatoes that are bruised, cracked, are sprouting their eyes, or are mottled with green patches. These poor-quality potatoes will spoil and discolor quicker and will taste bitter.

How to handle. Potatoes are a hearty and rugged vegetable, but handle them gently because they do bruise easily. Store them in a cool, dark, well-ventilated place and they will keep for 10 days to 2 weeks. After that, they will begin to sprout their eyes, shrivel, and begin to deteriorate.

If you buy them in a paper bag, open the bag and be sure they get air. If they come in a plastic bag, remove them to a bin or paper bag for better ventilation.

Nutritional value. One medium potato with skin, about 150 grams or ⅓ pound, contains from 110 to 126 calories, 550 to 750 milligrams of potassium, and 40 percent of your daily requirement of vitamin C. It is also very high in fiber but contains no fat or cholesterol and very little sodium.

History and folklore. Potatoes are native to South America and are believed to have originated in the Andes Mountains of Peru as early as 3000 B.C. The Spanish brought potatoes back to Europe, where they were at first distrusted as a food source, mainly because they were new and people were accustomed to eating parsnips and turnips, but also because potatoes grown in Europe in those days occasionally contained high doses of solanine, a toxic substance that can cause illness. But Europeans soon realized that potatoes were an inexpensive, nutritious, and easy-to-grow food source for expanding populations.

How to grow. Potatoes are grown from other potatoes. Nurseries and seed companies cut seed potatoes into "sets," which can be planted in a well-tilled, well-drained soil in early spring, 2 weeks before the last frost. Harvest new potatoes as soon as the tubers appear. Harvest mature potatoes 2 weeks after their vines have died.

RADISHES

Except for the large Japanese radish called daikon, radishes are the one root that is rarely ever cooked. Most people simply eat them raw sprinkled with a little salt. The piquancy of radishes varies from one type to another, but, in general, young, fresh radishes are crisp, tender, and sweet, with only a hint of hotness.

In addition to the tiny round red radish, look for white icicle radishes, the finger-long white-tipped French breakfast radish, the all-white round radish, and the turnip-sized black radish that is as hot as horseradish. Farmers' markets are good places to find these varieties, especially the Easter Egg radishes, which come in hues of red, pink, white, and even purple.

Daikon radish should be about 6 to 8 inches long and about 1½ inches thick. It is not uncommon to find daikon that is much larger than this. Feel free to use them because even huge daikons are sweet and crispy. They will grow larger, but the younger ones are more tender. They are perfectly tasty and crunchy simply sliced and added to an appetizer tray, but in Asian cuisines they are shredded, sliced, and stir-fried or marinated with hot pepper sauces and eaten as a Korean relish called kim chee.

Another new radish on the market is radish sprouts. These ultra-thin tangy sprouts are perfect for sandwiches or as decoration on a crudité platter. Look for daikon sprouts for their extra-spicy flavor and extended length.

How to buy. Look for radishes that still have their tops attached. Green fresh-looking tops means that the radishes are fresh and at their peak. If the radishes are topped and packaged in plastic, look inside to be sure the radishes are clean, firm, and smooth fleshed with no hint of drying or discoloration.

Daikons usually are sold individually, sometimes with their stems still intact and, occasionally, if they are small, tied in a bunch of three. Look for smooth white skin with a pale hint of green that is smooth and clean with no cuts or blemishes.

Radish sprouts are almost always sold in square, transparent, pop-open plastic boxes. Daikon sprout boxes are taller and more rectangular.

How to handle. Wash radishes to remove any grit. They will keep for up to a week wrapped in plastic and placed in the refrigerator, but it is much better to eat them within 2 or 3 days.

Sprouts are very perishable. Store them in the refrigerator and use within 1 or 2 days.

Nutritional value. Radishes and radish sprouts are very low in calories and sodium and contain only trace amounts of vitamins and minerals.

History and folklore. Long before people used forks and knives, radishes were grown and enjoyed by people around the world. They are known to have been eaten by the ancient Chinese and the ancient Egyptians, Romans, and Greeks.

How to grow. Radishes are probably the easiest vegetable to grow. They are especially fun for children to grow because they always sprout and are ready to eat in as little as 20 to 25 days. Every garden catalogue and seed store has a large selection of radish seeds.

Simply plant radishes in spring as soon as the ground can be tilled. Continue planting more every 2 weeks for a continuous supply all summer long. Plant black radishes in summer for a fall harvest.

RUTABAGA

The poet Carl Sandburg writes about his days as a boy growing up around Galesburg, Illinois, and seeing horse-drawn wagons full of rutabagas heading off to market. This makes sense because Galesburg was settled by people of Scandinavian heritage and rutabagas are oftentimes called Swedish turnips.

This heavy orange root is probably among the most valuable of all vegetables. It is very high in vitamins and minerals, it is very inexpensive, it keeps well and is available all year round, and it is easy to cook and very delicious. It has an earthy, honest flavor and is never bitter as turnips can be.

How to buy. Look for rutabagas in the bins next to the potatoes at the market. They are round and about the size of a large grapefruit or softball. They are light brown to orange and often touched with purple at the very top. One medium rutabaga will feed a family of four as a side dish because there is very little waste.

How to handle. Rutabagas are often wrapped in a thin coating of wax. Simply peel this off at the same time that you peel off the thin coating of skin. You will need a large, heavy knife to slice the root because it is very heavy and dense. The simplest way to try rutabaga the first time is to chop it, boil it for 10 to 15 minutes, strain, and serve with butter, salt, and pepper. Its texture is very much like potatoes. A rutabaga will keep for up to a month if kept in a cool, dry place.

Nutritional value. The orange flesh of rutabaga means that it is very high in beta carotene, which turns into vitamin A, which is thought to be a factor in preventing cancer. It is also a member of the cruciferous cabbage family, which is also thought to help prevent certain types of cancer.

One-half cup of cooked rutabaga contains only 35 calories, 4 milligrams of sodium, and no fat or cholesterol. It has 550 units of vitamin A, 167 milligrams of potassium, and up to 40 milligrams of vitamin C.

History and folklore. Rutabaga has always lived in the shadow of its turnip twin. Turnips were eaten by primitive people in both China and Europe, as witnessed by their drawings of turnips on their cave walls. The commercially grown rutabaga we find in the market today is the result of cross-breeding a turnip with a cabbage.

Wisconsin and Minnesota, states with cool climates and large populations of Scandinavians and Germans, are the main producers of rutabaga in the United States, but most of the rutabaga we eat comes from Canada.

How to grow. Rutabagas will grow in any fertile, well-tilled soil in the cooler climates of the United States and Canada. American

Purple Top is a popular variety that takes 90 days to mature from seed planted in the early summer.

SALSIFY AND SCORZONERA

Salsify and its black-skinned cousin are both long, tapering roots that are not widely grown or made available in the United States. You might find some at farmers' markets. Those you find in the market have likely been imported from Europe, where they are better appreciated.

Salsify is sometimes called oyster plant because the flavor somewhat resembles oysters, but also asparagus and even artichoke bottoms. The flavor and texture of salsify and scorzonera are similar.

How to buy. Look for roots that are similar in size and shape to carrots and parsnips. They should be clean and firm and free from blemishes and cuts.

How to handle. Wash, trim, and peel salsify and scorzonera and use them in soups, stews, and casseroles. They have a delicate flavor that is best displayed simply steamed and lightly buttered.

Nutritional value. Both roots are very low in calories, only about 35 for 100 grams, and they are a good source of fiber.

History and folklore. Both of these roots were probably dug up from the wild and eaten for food for centuries. They were first cultivated in Europe in the sixteenth and seventeenth centuries.

How to grow. Because salsify and scorzonera are rarities in the market, if you are determined to enjoy them at their best, you might try growing some. Since these roots are rather long, it might be best to grow them in a raised bed so that the soil is sufficiently deep and crumbly. Mammoth Sandwich Island is the common variety of salsify and Giant Black Russian is the common variety of scorzonera.

SWEET POTATOES

Sweet potatoes and yams are two different and distinct vegetables. The brown-skinned, orange-fleshed sweet potato that Americans love to eat candied at Thanksgiving is *Ipomoea batatas,* a potatolike tuber that is a member of the morning glory family, which is native to Central America and the Caribbean. A true yam is a *Dioscorea bulbifera,* an elongated brown-skinned, white-fleshed root that is native to Africa.

Africans who came to the New World as slaves called their yams nyami. When they found sweet potatoes to eat, they called them nyami, too. Soon everyone began calling sweet potatoes yams. True yams from Africa began to be cultivated in the Caribbean, and they are now one of the most popular foods there.

But now true yams are becoming common in American markets, and it is important to distinguish between sweet potatoes and true yams. Finally, the flesh of a sweet potato is sometimes more golden or yellow than deep orange. This yellow color is just a minor variation on the basic orange sweet potato.

How to buy. Choose smooth-skinned sweet potatoes of medium size that are tapered at the ends. Avoid ones that have blemishes, have been cut, or have skin that is beginning to shrivel and dry. North Carolina, Virginia, and Louisiana are the leading producers of sweet potatoes in the United States.

Sweet potatoes are available year-round, but they are at their best and most available from September through January.

How to handle. Sweet potatoes are fairly perishable. Keep them in a cool, dark, dry place and they will store well for up to 2 weeks. Do not refrigerate them because it makes them tough.

Sweet potatoes are excellent baked or microwaved with their jackets on, then split and buttered. They can be boiled and mashed and added to flour to make pies, cakes, and muffins. If you slice them to make stir-fries or home fries, be sure to use a stainless steel knife to avoid discoloration.

Nutritional value. Sweet potatoes are a powerhouse of health and nutrition. One medium baked sweet potato provides twice the daily requirement of vitamin A, about a third of the daily requirement of vitamin C, yet it contains only 114 calories, about the same as a glass of orange juice.

History and folklore. Sweet potatoes are native American plants found by Columbus as he sailed the Caribbean. Indians in Central and South America and Louisiana also grew sweet potatoes. Spanish and Portuguese explorers took the plants to Asia and back to Europe.

Europe's climate was too cool to grow sweet potatoes, but they grew quite well in the early Virginia colonies. They have been a popular vegetable throughout the United States ever since.

How to grow. Sweet potatoes require a long, very warm growing season, making them more suitable to the southern United States. Sweet potatoes are grown from plants created by taking cuttings from other sweet potato vines or roots. Plant the sprouts in a warm, fertile soil and harvest in 110 to 120 days.

TURNIPS

Turnips have an undeserved bad reputation in this country because people think they are bitter and that they have to be boiled with sugar to taste good enough to eat. Those people have probably been eating tough old woody turnips that are too large and past their prime. Fresh young turnips picked at the right stage are tender, sweet, crunchy, and delicious.

How to buy. Turnips sold in markets usually are displayed with their green tops already cut off, whether in bulk or in 1-pound plastic bags. Look for nicely rounded turnips, the size of a tangerine or large lemon. Smaller sizes are better if you can find them. Look for smooth, unblemished skin that is white and often tinged with purple at the top. The best months for buying turnips are October through March in supermarkets and early summer in farmers' markets.

How to handle. If the turnips are fresh and tender, all you need to do is wash them. Some people like to peel off a thin layer of the slightly fibrous outer flesh to get to the tender inner flesh. Turnips should be used within 3 to 5 days.

Nutritional value. Turnips are members of the cruciferous cabbage family, which is thought to be a factor in preventing cancer. A cup of cooked, diced turnips, which has only about 30 calories, contains one-half the daily requirement of vitamin C and 268 milligrams of potassium.

History and folklore. Turnips are native to Siberia and Europe, especially those northern countries of Germany, France, and Scandinavia. The Romans were growing turnips by the year A.D. 42, but the English did not begin to grow them until the middle of the sixteenth century. Henry VIII was known to be a great fan of turnips, which were eaten roasted over coals in those days. The French explorer Jacques Cartier planted turnips in Canada in 1540, and Thomas Jefferson was just one of hundreds of American colonists who planted and ate turnips.

How to grow. Turnips grow best when they grow fast. They prefer the cool, moist conditions of early spring and early fall.

Plant turnips as soon as the ground can be worked in spring, and in late August in fall. Thin them relentlessly so that the roots have room to grow. Harvest them when they are very young.

TURNIP GREENS

Turnip greens are the verdant, feathery tops of turnip roots. The turnip greens you find in the supermarket have already had their roots cut off. They are an outstanding source of vitamin A and are very tasty when chopped and added to stews and soups.

How to buy. Look for fresh green leaves that have not started to wilt. They usually come tied in bunches next to the collard, kale, or mustard greens.

How to handle. Wash turnip greens thoroughly because sand and grit can get embedded in their crinkled leaves. Wrapped in a plastic bag, they will stay fresh in the refrigerator for 2 to 3 days.

The traditional use of turnip greens was to boil them in salted water for several hours along with a bit of bacon or salt pork. This indeed is a savory dish but is not all turnips have to offer. Young tender turnip greens, usually found in farmers' markets or in African-American neighborhoods where greens are much admired, can be chopped, steamed, and served with butter or vinegar in as little as 5 minutes. Turnip greens are also good chopped and added to soups and stews or stir-fried.

Nutritional value. One cup of turnip greens contains one and a half times the daily requirement of vitamin C and almost twice the recommended daily requirement of vitamin A. It has only 20 calories.

History and folklore. Turnip greens have been eaten as long as turnip roots. They are traditionally a dish loved by people in southern states, where the liquid from simmered greens used to be considered an elixir or spring tonic.

How to grow. If you grow turnips, you can harvest turnip greens when you thin the rows or harvest the young turnip roots. Young turnips and turnip greens are delicious cooked together.

CARIBBEAN ROOTS

As more people from Jamaica, the Dominican Republic, Puerto Rico, Trinidad, and Cuba become citizens of the United States and find jobs and homes in cities and towns all over, their favored foods are sure to follow. The same thing has happened with all immigrant groups, giving us food finds such as Polish sausages, Italian broccoli, Chinese stir-fries—the list goes on and on.

One of the biggest problems identifying Caribbean roots is that several languages are spoken in the Caribbean and each group may call a root a different name. Cassava is also known as yuca and manioc, for instance. Furthermore, some of these roots look alike, making it even more difficult to make choices for cooking. Luckily, names and looks don't matter very much because they all have a similar starchy quality and they are easily used interchangeably for the most part. Just think of them as slightly more exotic than sweet potatoes.

Nutritionally, Caribbean roots have about as many calories as potatoes. They are low in salt and high in fiber and complex carbohydrates.

Don't bother trying to grow these roots unless you live in South Florida or the Caribbean itself. But there these roots are so cheap and plentiful it doesn't pay to grow them.

Instead, look for them to be stacked next to the potatoes and onions in the produce section of your supermarket or go the extra mile and search them out in Hispanic or Jamaican produce markets, where the people who work and shop there can tell you how to cook and eat them.

Boniato

Also known as batata, white sweet potato, or Cuban sweet potato. Boniato is a lumpy, rounded sweet potato with pinkish-red skin and white flesh. It is just as sweet but a little drier than our orange sweet potato. It can be microwaved, baked, mashed, or fried and used in soups, stews, or anywhere you would use potato. One cup contains 220 calories and over 400 milligrams of potassium. Boniato is probably the easiest to enjoy for the Caribbean root novice, so try it first before you go on to any others.

Cassava

Also known as yuca or manioc. These roots range in size from 6 to 12 inches long, and 1 to 3 inches in diameter. Their brown skin is barklike and often coated with wax. People around the world in tropical climates have eaten these as a starchy staple called tapioca. It has a white, mild-flavored flesh that is a little bit coarse. Peel and cook in stews, soups, mashed, or fried. One cup contains 270 calories and some iron.

Malanga

Also known as yautia or tannier. These roots are 6 to 8 inches long and slightly tapered at one end. The skin is shaggy and brown and the flesh is beige with a taste slightly sweeter than white potatoes. It is an important starch food source for tropical people all over the world. Boil it and use it in potato salads, soups, stews, or buttered with salt and pepper. One cup of malanga contains about 270 calories.

Taro

Also known as eddo or dasheen. It is often confused with malanga because it has the same shaggy brown skin. But taro's flesh is whiter than malanga and it is usually shorter and more round.

Taro is the edible root of the plant that produces callaloo, the leafy green spinachlike vegetable that is used in soups in the Caribbean. Taro roots can be peeled and cooked like potatoes. They have a flavor reminiscent of chestnuts.

Yam

Also known as batata, yampi, name, igmane, cush-cush, and other names. The true Caribbean yam is nothing like the American sweet potato, which is often incorrectly called yam. Yam is the most widely eaten tuberous root in the Caribbean and probably in Africa and tropical Asia. It comes in various shapes and sizes but is commonly 6 to 10 inches long and 2 to 3 inches wide. The skin is shaggy and brown and the flesh is white and slightly slippery. It is good fried like potato chips or boiled and used as a base for spicy stews. One cup contains 80 calories and good amounts of potassium.

ROOT SPICES

Ginger

Gingersnaps flavored with dried ginger powder is about as close to this wonderful food as many people get. That's unfortunate, because fresh ginger adds zip and unique flavor to foods when used as a condiment.

How to buy. Chinese people use large amounts of ginger in their cooking, and they are very particular about the quality of the ginger they buy. It is always such a treat to shop the open-air green markets of New York's Chinatown and buy the freshest, juicy aromatic ginger in the world.

Fresh ginger is very common in supermarket produce aisles. They look like gnarled "hands" with several "fingers" all covered with a thin light-brown skin. Choose ginger "hands" that have fleshy palms and stubby "fingers." Pick ones that are bright, fresh looking, and firm, with no signs of shriveling.

How to handle. When a recipe calls for fresh ginger, simply slice off a section from the whole, peel it, and slice or mince it with a sharp knife. The remainder of the ginger will "heal" its cut and remain fresh until the next time you want to use it. Stored in a plastic container in the refrigerator, it will keep for a week to 10 days.

Nutritional value. Ginger does have trace elements of many vitamins and minerals, but because you use so little of it at a time, it is pointless to rely on ginger for those nutrients.

History and folklore. Ginger is a creeping perennial that is considered to be a native of tropical Southeast Asia. Since ancient times it has spread to China, India, the Mediterranean, and finally to the West Indies, where ginger beer is a very popular drink.

How to grow. Climate makes it pointless to try to grow ginger in the United States—with the exception of Hawaii. Most of our ginger is imported from Central America.

Horseradish

The following is part of a story I wrote for the *New York Daily News,* published on April 1, 1987.

> "Horseradish for Passover has to be bitter so that you will feel bitter when you eat it," says Sol Kaplan, the cashier and resident expert on Jewish culture and tradition at Guss's Pickles on Essex Street on New York's Lower East Side.
>
> "It has to be so bitter that it brings tears to your eyes, so that you keep crying, so you can remember your years in slavery," he adds.
>
> Guss's Pickles and the other pickle stores in New York's old Jewish quarter grate over 1,000 pounds of fresh horseradish, usu-

ally on a hand-cranked grater right before their customer's eyes, every year for Passover. Bert Blitz, the manager of Guss's, says that when he buys his horseradish he looks for heavier roots, "about the size of your forearm because they are older and more flavorful."

He says if you are buying your own, look for roots that are firm but not dried out. You can grate it with a food processor at home but a cheese grater will work just fine. Just wash it, peel it and grate it.

How to buy. Horseradish looks like a cross between a club and an old femur bone the dog dragged in. But it is neither of those. It is simply a pungent root that grows underground. It has a pale brown skin and white flesh.

As Bert Blitz said, look for roots that are firm and heavy, that are unblemished and look and smell fresh. Fresh horseradish is most common around Passover but is also available in fall and winter months.

If you can't find fresh horseradish, you can always use the prepared variety that is packed in vinegar and jarred. Sometimes prepared horseradish has vegetable oil and flavorings added to it. Be sure to drain and rinse prepared horseradish to reveal its best flavor.

How to handle. Fresh horseradish can be wrapped in plastic and stored in the refrigerator for a month or more. Simply grate it as you need it. You can always grate it and pack it in vinegar if you find it takes up too much room in the fridge.

Eastern European Jewish families traditionally eat horseradish with gefilte fish at Passover, and we are all aware of horseradish in spicy shrimp cocktail sauce. But horseradish is a popular condiment to eat with roast beef in England. Polish and other Slavic cooks add horseradish to veal dishes, and Hungarians eat their delicious pork sausages with horseradish, never with mustard.

History and folklore. Horseradish originated in Eastern Europe and Western Asia, but it has spread throughout most countries of Northern Europe, Scandinavia, and the United Kingdom. An Illinois farming area near the Illinois and Mississippi rivers, north of St.

Louis, bills itself as the "Horseradish Capital of the World," and that is indeed where most American horseradish is grown. New Jersey, Wisconsin, and other states also produce horseradish.

Nutritional value. Horseradish is not known as a significant source of vitamins and minerals but it is low in salt and calories.

Grow your own. Horseradish is easy to grow, maybe too easy. It is a hardy, wandering perennial that will invade other parts of your garden if not confined. Simply plant horseradish roots in early spring in any rich, well-drained soil. The J. W. Jung Seed Company of Randolph, Wisconsin, sells a nifty horseradish root called Bohemian.

Antipasto, Appetizers, Crudités, and Canapés

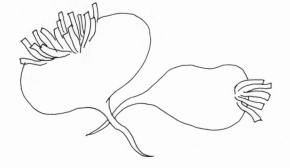

E ven though root vegetables are nutritious, delicious, and reasonably priced, not every member of every family is familiar with their good qualities. In fact, roots, especially some of the unusual ones, may seem a little exotic.

That certainly isn't the case. Most everyone has eaten and enjoyed radishes, and certainly carrots are universally popular. To get your family to try some additional roots might take a little coaxing and even some trickery.

Whenever cooks try to get people to eat an unfamiliar meat dish, they invariably say, "It tastes like chicken." Well, with roots such as jicama or daikon, you might say they taste just like radishes. To get them to try rutabaga, say they taste just like potatoes. They can't disagree, and once they have tried it, they'll like it.

Appetizers, antipasto, canapés, and crudités are good ways to get your friends and family to try a little bite of a new root they haven't eaten before or think they ate once in childhood and didn't like.

This chapter will give recipes for an international assortment of crudité or raw vegetable platters, raw and grilled vegetable appetizers, canapé sandwiches, tapas, finger foods, and other "little bites" of roots. All of the recipes are designed for small family gatherings of 4 to 6 people but can easily be doubled or tripled if you are planning to entertain a larger crowd.

Even though many of these recipes are grouped into culinary categories, feel free to pick and choose any recipe and serve it any way you like. Anything goes as long as people eat more roots.

The Crudité Family

Crudité is a simple assortment of raw vegetables served with dips or tossed with salad dressings that is popular in many cultures. Here is a gathering of crudité and appetizer plates of American, French, Russian, Italian, and Spanish origin and influence rounded out with a few side dishes tossed in.

The American Crudité Platter

The most important things to remember about an American buffet-style crudité platter are that the vegetables must be fresh, they must be cut into manageable slices, and the dips should not drip or run. And you want your guests to eat it. So, it must be colorful, enticing, well arranged, and inviting. Placing a few different roots on the tray helps spark their attention and perk up their appetites.

People already look forward to finding carrots and radishes in crudité, but did you know that sweet potato, jicama, daikon, turnip, and radish sprouts are outstanding additions?

> *1 to 2 each carrot, cucumber, sweet potato*
> *1 each jicama and daikon radish*
> *Sweet green, red, yellow, or brown bell pepper*
> *1 bunch or bag red radishes*
> *1 box radish or daikon sprouts*

1. Peel the carrot, cucumber, sweet potato, jicama, and daikon. Slice into sticks 2½ to 3 inches long and ¼ inch thick. Remove the seeds from the bell pepper and slice into ¼-inch-wide strips. Wash and trim the radishes. Wrap all vegetables in plastic and refrigerate until ready to use.

2. Arrange the vegetables on a platter in groups, alternating colors. Remove the radish sprouts from the box, wash, and drain. Place

clumps of radish sprouts in between the vegetable groups, around the edges of the plate, and in the center as garnish.

3. Keep the platter covered with plastic and refrigerated until the guests arrive. Take the platter out at the last minute and serve with the following dips.

HORSERADISH AND YOGURT DIP

> *2 cups unflavored yogurt*
> *2 tablespoons mayonnaise*
> *2 tablespoons freshly grated or prepared horse-*
> *radish*

Combine all the ingredients, stir well, and serve.

TAPENADE

> *1 clove garlic, peeled and chopped*
> *2 small anchovy fillets that have been rinsed in*
> *water to remove excess salt*
> *1 whole egg*
> *4 or 5 dried black olives, pitted (substitute any black*
> *olive of your choice)*
> *Juice of ½ lemon, about 1 tablespoon*
> *1 cup olive oil or other salad oil*

1. Place the garlic, anchovy fillets, egg, olives, and lemon juice in a blender or food processor. Process to a smooth creamy purée.

2. With the blender running at low speed, slowly add the olive oil a few drops at a time to create a thick, mayonnaiselike dip.

3. Remove from the blender and place in a serving bowl. Garnish with a black olive or an anchovy fillet to alert your guests to the flavors.

HUMMUS

1 16- to 19-ounce can chickpeas, a.k.a. garbanzo or
  ceci beans
½ cup tahini sesame butter
1 small clove garlic, chopped (optional)
Juice of 1 lemon, about 2 tablespoons
¼ cup fruity olive oil (extra-virgin is best for this)

1. Drain the chickpeas and rinse them under cold water. Reserve the chickpea liquid. Place the chickpeas in a blender or food processor.

2. Add the tahini, garlic, lemon juice, and olive oil to the blender. Process until you achieve a smooth creamy paste. You may have to add a little of the reserved chickpea liquid to the mixture if it is too dry.

NORTH CAROLINA SWEET POTATO DIP

1 pint sour cream
¾ cup dark brown sugar
½ teaspoon cinnamon, or to taste
⅛ teaspoon nutmeg, or to taste

Place all ingredients in a small mixing bowl and stir to blend well. Keep covered and refrigerated until time to serve. Place it near the sweet potatoes or make a separate serving arrangement of the sweet potatoes and their sweet dip.

If your party or gathering is featuring a Mexican, Tex-Mex, southwestern entrée, or maybe just a big pot of chili and cornbread, try these salsas dipped with jicama slices.

TOMATILLO SALSA VERDE

4 to 5 fresh, whole, husked or 1 cup drained canned
  tomatillos, chopped
1 small red Spanish onion, peeled and chopped
2 small jalapeño or serrano chilies, seeded and
  chopped
2 tablespoons chopped fresh cilantro

Place all ingredients in a blender or food processor and blend to a smooth sauce, 2 to 3 quick pulses for a processor and 20 to 30 seconds for a blender.

SALSA CRUDA

1 pound fresh tomatoes or 1 28-ounce can, peeled,
  seeded, and chopped
3 fresh or canned serrano or jalapeño chilies, seeded
  and chopped
1 medium onion, peeled and chopped
2 tablespoons chopped fresh cilantro
2 cloves garlic, peeled and chopped

Place all ingredients in a blender or food processor and blend to a smooth sauce, 2 to 3 quick pulses for a processor and 30 seconds for a blender.

French Assiette des Crudités

Assiette des crudités, or assorted raw vegetables, is a common first-course offering at restaurants in France, especially those that cater to budget-minded families and students. It is a staple first course of prix fixe menus. This assiette features carrots, beets, French potato salad, and céleri-rave rémoulade. With the addition of a small wedge of pâté, it makes an ideal light lunch.

To serve an assiette des crudités, spoon the salads onto individual plates in separate mounds. Place a leaf of Belgian endive between each mound and fill the endive with individual pieces of different pâté. Serve with French bread, cornichon pickles, and cold white wine.

CARROTS IN DILLED VINAIGRETTE

2 to 3 fresh raw carrots
1 ounce red wine vinegar
1 tablespoon Dijon or country mustard
½ tablespoon fresh or ½ teaspoon dry dill weed
Salt and freshly ground black pepper to taste
3 ounces olive oil or other salad oil

1. Wash and peel the carrots and shred them into the finest grate your mandoline, grater, or food processor can manage.

2. Make the vinaigrette by whisking or blending together the vinegar, mustard, dill, salt, and pepper. Slowly add the oil and whisk to form a creamy dressing. If pressed for time or for convenience' sake, you can substitute any good-quality bottled vinaigrette.

3. Add the carrots to the vinaigrette and stir to blend well. Let this mixture rest for the flavors to mingle for 15 to 30 minutes.

BEETS WITH CARAWAY AND OIL

2 to 3 medium fresh raw beets
3 tablespoons walnut, hazelnut, olive, or other
*   salad oil*
1 teaspoon caraway seeds
Salt and pepper to taste

1. Wash and peel the beets. Shred them fine and place them in a small bowl.

2. Add the walnut or other oil, the caraway seeds, salt, and pepper to the beets. Stir and let rest for 15 to 30 minutes before serving.

FRENCH POTATO SALAD TARRAGON

10 small or 5 red or white new potatoes
¾ cup prepared mayonnaise
1 tablespoon white tarragon vinegar
1 tablespoon fresh or 1 teaspoon dry tarragon leaves
2 shallots, peeled and minced
Salt and freshly ground black pepper to taste

1. Wash the potatoes and place them in a medium pot with water to cover and boil until tender, about 20 minutes. Drain and cool.

2. Peel the potatoes and chop them into ½-inch cubes. Place them in a medium mixing bowl.

3. Blend the mayonnaise, the tarragon vinegar, the tarragon, the shallots, salt, and pepper in a medium mixing bowl.

4. Combine the dressing with the potatoes, folding carefully in order not to break up the potatoes. Serve with a garnish of fresh tarragon leaves.

CÉLERI-RAVE RÉMOULADE

2 medium or 1 large celery root
1 cup good-quality mayonnaise
1 to 2 teaspoons fresh lemon juice
1 tablespoon Dijon mustard
1 to 2 tablespoons fresh minced chervil or parsley
   (do not use dried)
Salt and pepper to taste

1. Wash and peel the celery root. Cut it into large sections, place in a large pot, and cover with water. Bring the water to a boil and simmer for 10 minutes. Drain and plunge celeriac into cold water. Drain and reserve.

2. Grate the celery root into medium-sized shreds. Place it into a medium mixing bowl.

3. In a separate mixing bowl, stir together the mayonnaise, lemon

juice, mustard, herbs, salt, and pepper. Combine the celery root and dressing and stir to blend well.

Russian Zakuski

Russians are fond of spending entire evenings in restaurant/nightclubs, surrounded by their friends and family, singing, dancing, drinking vodka, and eating an endless procession of zakuski, or appetizers. Black radish, parsnip latkes with caviar, and beets are featured here.

People at Russian tables love to interact with each other, so serve the salads and other foods of the zakuski in separate bowls or plates and have guests pass them around. Serve with good-quality rye bread, pickled herring, smoked salmon and sturgeon, caviar, thin slices of beef tongue and horseradish, and lots of ice-cold flavored vodka.

COLD BEET CUPS STUFFED
WITH HERBED CHEESE

> *4 large or 6 to 8 small beets, washed and trimmed*
> *6 ounces cream cheese, farmer's cheese, fresh goat*
> * cheese, even cottage cheese or ricotta*
> *2 tablespoons minced fresh herbs such as chives,*
> * dill, or parsley or a combination of these.*
> * (Here you can easily substitute a spreadable pre-*
> * pared herbed cheese found in a supermarket*
> * cheese section.)*
> *Salt and pepper to taste*

1. Place the beets in a large pot of water, bring to a boil, turn the heat to medium, and simmer for 35 minutes. Drain and cool.

2. Peel the beets and cut the large ones in half. Use a spoon and scoop out the insides of the beets to form little cups.

---

3. Place the beet scooping in a food processor. Add the cheese, herbs, salt, and pepper. Pulse to form a smooth paste.

4. Fill the beet cups with the paste and refrigerate for 30 minutes before serving.

BLACK RADISH WITH ONION

1 large black radish, about ¾ pound
2 fresh green scallions
1 cup sour cream
2 tablespoons fresh minced chives (optional)
Salt and pepper to taste

1. Wash and peel the black radish. Grate it medium-fine and place in a medium saucepan. Cover with water, bring to a boil, simmer for 2 minutes, drain and cool.

NOTE: If you can't get black radish, you can substitute daikon or even small red ones. If you have to substitute, omit the cooking process. Simply grate the radishes, but add a tablespoon of freshly grated or prepared horseradish to give the dish a bitter jolt.

2. Trim and finely chop the scallions, including the green tops. Blend the grated radishes with the sour cream, scallions, chives, salt and pepper to taste. Refrigerate and let rest for 20 minutes before serving.

PARSNIP LATKES WITH CAVIAR AND SOUR CREAM

2 large potatoes
2 parsnips
2 eggs
2 tablespoons all-purpose flour
½ teaspoon salt
Freshly ground black pepper to taste
Oil for frying
Sour cream and caviar

1. Peel and grate the potatoes and parsnips and place them in a muslin or lightweight cotton towel. Squeeze out as much moisture as possible. Place the potatoes and parsnips in a large mixing bowl and toss to combine.

2. Mix the eggs, flour, salt, and pepper in a separate bowl and stir to blend well. Add to the roots mixture.

3. Pour ¼ cup of oil into a large, heavy frying pan and heat over medium-high. Place tablespoonfuls of latke mixture in the hot oil and fry until golden brown. Keep the cooked latkes warm in the oven until all are done.

4. Serve the latkes hot, topped with sour cream and caviar. You will need about 1 pound of sour cream, but it is hard to determine how much caviar you can afford and how much your guests can eat.

Bagna Cauda and Pinzimonio Antipasto

The diet of Italians has been touted as very healthy in recent years because it is high in fresh vegetables and olive oil. Pinzimonio is a dish of raw vegetables dipped in olive oil. Bagna cauda is a dish of raw vegetables dipped in a hot anchovy-flavored bath. There is no reason why pinzimonio and bagna cauda shouldn't be served at the same time.

Italian restaurants invariably have a groaning antipasto table full of tempting little plates of appetizers. Focaccia, here topped with parsnip shards, is often part of an Italian antipasto platter. Serve these dishes as part of an Italian buffet or accompany with salami and cheese for a tasty lunch or picnic al fresco.

For both pinzimonio and bagna cauda you need a large assortment of vegetables. The traditional Italian varieties include zucchini, red and green bell pepper, artichoke bottoms, broccoli stalks, celery, and fennel. For four people, you will need about 1 cup of each of those vegetables sliced into sticks. Now add:

3 medium carrots, peeled and sliced into sticks
1 bunch red radishes, washed and trimmed
1 cup of either jicama or daikon cut into sticks
1 bunch fresh scallions, trimmed
1 to 2 cups sweet onion slices

PINZIMONIO

½ cup extra-virgin Italian olive oil
½ teaspoon kosher or table salt
½ teaspoon freshly ground black pepper
1 teaspoon fresh lemon juice

1. In a small mixing bowl, combine all the ingredients. Transfer to one large or several tiny serving bowls.

2. Place the vegetables on a large serving platter. People can pick and choose the types of vegetables they like and then dip them in the flavored olive oil pinzimonio.

NOTE: Olive oils vary in flavor and color depending on whether they come from Sicily, France, Italy, Spain, or California. Amastra from Sicily is very dark green and fruity, while Provençal oil is light and refined. Also, try dipping in walnut or hazelnut oil, available at gourmet groceries.

BAGNA CAUDA

¾ cup fruity olive oil
3 tablespoons sweet butter
2 large cloves garlic, peeled and minced
8 anchovy fillets, chopped

1. Gather and prepare the same collection of vegetables as you did for pinzimonio. Place on a large serving platter.

2. Heat the oil and butter in a medium saucepan over medium heat until the butter melts and begins to sizzle. Add the garlic and

cook for 1 minute. Add the anchovy fillets and cook, smashing the anchovies until they break up.

3. Pour the bagna cauda into an earthenware bowl and keep warm on a very low-heat hot plate or a fondue pot with a candle.

4. Guests should dip the vegetables in the hot oil with their fingers or with tiny forks.

FOCACCIA

Focaccia is really a large pizza pie baked without the tomato, cheese, and other toppings. Dozens of different types of pizza are made around the Mediterranean, and this is one of them.

> 1 package active dry yeast
> ½ cup lukewarm water
> 3 cups all-purpose flour, plus a little more for
>   kneading
> ½ cup water
> 2 teaspoons salt
> ½ cup olive oil
> 1 clove garlic, minced
> 3 shallots, peeled and finely sliced

1. Dissolve the yeast in ½ cup lukewarm water. Stir and let rest for 10 minutes.

2. In a large mixing bowl, combine the yeast mixture, the flour, water, and salt and stir to blend well. Knead for 10 minutes and place in a bowl that has been rubbed with oil. Let rise in a warm place for 1 hour.

3. Remove dough from the bowl and knead in ¼ cup olive oil. Return to the bowl and let rise in a warm place for 30 minutes.

4. Remove dough from bowl and roll out to fit into a 12-by-18-inch baking pan. Press your fingers into the dough to form little indentations. Sprinkle the garlic, shallots, and remaining olive oil over the dough.

5. Bake in a 400°F oven for 15 to 20 minutes. Remove, cut into squares, and serve.

Spanish Tapas

Most people are aware now of the Spanish custom of meeting friends in bars after work, drinking beer, wine, or sipping sherry and snacking on appetizers known as tapas. Tortilla Español, which is really a big potato-and-egg omelet, and potato salad are always part of the assortment.

Tortilla Español is cut into wedges like pie or cake to be served and Tapas Roots Salad is served like any other potato salad. Accompany these dishes with black and green olives, toasted almonds, dried serrano ham or dry fuet sausage, grilled chorizo, and plenty of napkins.

TORTILLA ESPAÑOL

> *1 medium Spanish onion, peeled and chopped fine*
> *½ cup plus 2 tablespoons olive oil*
> *1 clove garlic, peeled and minced*
> *4 large Kennebec-type white potatoes, peeled and*
>   *cut into thin slices*
> *6 large eggs*
> *Salt and pepper to taste*

1. In a heavy 9-inch skillet, sauté the onion in ½ cup olive oil over medium heat for 5 minutes. Add the minced garlic and potato slices, cover the skillet, and continue cooking for 20 minutes. Keep the heat low to avoid browning the potatoes.

2. Combine the eggs, salt, and pepper in a large mixing bowl. Beat the eggs until they are foamy. Remove the potatoes and onions from the pan and mix them in with the eggs.

3. Scrape the skillet clean with a spatula and return it to medium or medium-low heat. Add the remaining 2 tablespoons olive oil. Pour the potato-and-egg mixture into the pan, spreading it around to form a nice flat cake.

4. When the eggs begin to set and the potatoes begin to brown on the bottom, place a plate facedown over the rim of the skillet. Invert the skillet and the plate, allowing the potato omelet to drop onto the plate. Slide the omelet back into the skillet, browned side up, and brown the other side. Cook another 3 to 5 minutes over low heat.

5. Remove the tortilla from the skillet, cover, and let rest. Slice into small party wedges and serve at room temperature.

TAPAS ROOTS SALAD

3 large carrots, peeled and diced
2 medium turnips, peeled and diced
1 small celery root, peeled and diced
1 large red or white all-purpose potato, peeled and diced
2 large beets
2 cups good-quality mayonnaise
2 tablespoons fruity olive oil
2 tablespoons Spanish sherry vinegar
1 small tin anchovy fillets
1 small jar whole roasted pimientos, sliced

1. Place the peeled and diced carrots, turnips, celery root, and potato in a large pan. Cover with water and simmer until just barely tender. Drain and cool.

2. Place the beets in a saucepan with water to cover. Simmer until tender, about 15 minutes. Cool, peel, and dice.

3. In a large mixing bowl, combine the mayonnaise, olive oil, and vinegar, and stir to blend well. Add the vegetables to the dressing and stir to blend well.

4. Form the salad into a smooth mound on a flat plate or platter. Alternate thin strips of pimiento and anchovy fillets around the sides and over the top of the salad.

Canapés and Sandwiches

People can relate to sandwiches. People can relate to tiny sandwiches called canapés. People should be able to relate to sandwiches and canapés that have little bits of delicious roots tucked into them.

VEGETABLE PITA

> *3 to 4 whole fresh pita breads*
> *1 cup shredded daikon or jicama*
> *½ cup shredded carrots*
> *½ cup pickled beets, drained*
> *4 hard-cooked eggs, sliced*
> *1 cup plain yogurt*
> *2 tablespoons prepared horseradish*
> *¼ teaspoon ground cumin (optional)*
> *1 container radish sprouts*

1. Cut the pita breads in half to form semicircles. If they are less than totally fresh, warm them over an open flame on the stove or in the oven for 20 seconds.
2. Put little bits of daikon, carrot, beets, and eggs in each pita pocket.
3. Make a sauce by stirring together the yogurt, horseradish, and cumin. Spoon a little sauce on each sandwich and top with a bunch of radish sprouts.

FRENCH BAGUETTE AND
RADISH SANDWICH

> *1 to 2 long, thin French baguettes*
> *1 to 2 bunches fresh-picked radishes, either*
> *   long, thin, white-tipped French breakfast*
> *   radishes or small, round red ones*
> *¼ pound sweet unsalted butter*
> *Kosher salt*

1. Slice the baguettes into sandwich lengths 4 to 5 inches long. Split in half and open up.

2. Wash and trim the radishes and slice into thin strips or thin rounds.

3. Thickly spread the bread with the unsalted butter. Place the radishes on the buttered bread, sprinkle with kosher salt, close, and eat.

PUMPERNICKEL, HAM, AND
PICKLED BEET CANAPÉ

> *½ pound of very thin-sliced pumpernickel bread*
> *¼ pound cream cheese*
> *½ to ¾ pound thin-sliced boiled or baked ham*
> *1 jar or can pickled beets, drained*

Spread the pumpernickel bread with cream cheese. Add a layer of ham and top with pickled beet slices. Leave the sandwiches whole as open-faced Danish smorgasbord or cut the sandwiches into quarters for canapés.

SOURDOUGH, ROAST BEEF,
AND RADISH CANAPÉ

¼ pound unsalted sweet cream butter
½ pound sourdough or rye bread, thinly sliced
½ to ¾ pound rare roast beef, thinly sliced
1 bunch fresh radishes, grated

Spread the butter on the slices of bread. Top with roast beef and a tiny clump of radish. Cut into quarters and serve as canapés.

THREE

Chips, Frites, and Fritters

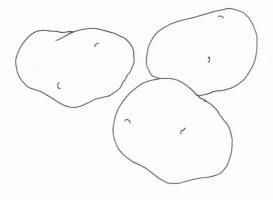

There's an old local culinary saying in Southern Illinois, "If you can't fry it, you can't eat it." That may be taking things to extremes, but people all over the world certainly do adore foods deep-fried in hot oil.

British people wouldn't think of eating their fish without their chips, which are really wedges of potato deep-fried right along with the fish. Frites are the precursors of American French fries, and no bistro in Paris would serve steak without a hearty platter of slender, skinny frites. And as the McDonald's Corporation has shown, French fries with hamburgers is probably America's favorite fast food.

But, recently, French fries have taken on new shapes and they are being made with roots other than potatoes. Chefs in New York and elsewhere have started making French fries and potato chips out of carrots, celeriac, parsnips, sweet potatoes, rutabaga, and Caribbean roots like yam and boniato.

This chapter is going to take a look at the wonderful world of deep-fried roots. Besides French fries and potato chips, you will learn to enjoy making onion rings, Japanese tempura and Italian fritto misto, fritters, egg rolls and wontons, even those cute little deep-fried potato baskets served in Chinese restaurants.

But, whoa there, buddy, aren't deep-fried foods laden with saturated fat, calories, and salt? The answer is yes, they are, but there are ways to mitigate the downside of these tasty foods.

First, always fry in vegetable oils that contain no saturated fats. Soy, safflower, canola, and peanut oil are all high in polyunsaturated fats. Canola oil is also high in monounsaturated fats that are considered to be beneficial in reducing certain cholesterol levels.

Second, always fry in oil that is at the correct heat, have the vegetables as dry as possible, and make sure they are at room temperature when frying begins. All of these techniques help prevent the food from absorbing any excess oil.

Finally, deep-frying will add excess fat to your diet no matter how hard you try to keep it out. That's why you shouldn't eat these foods if you are on a restricted fat-intake diet. Nor should you eat these foods very often. Once or twice a year is often enough to remind you of their wonderful flavors without adding extra fat to your diet.

All of the recipes in this section will feed 2 to 4 people.

FRITES, CHIPS, AND FRENCH-FRIED ROOTS

Frites, chips, and French fries are all the same food with different names. They are all small pieces of root vegetables deep-fried in hot oil. They are cut in different shapes and sizes to give them their flair and traditional appeal.

The ingredients: 3 to 4 medium Idaho or all-purpose white potatoes from Long Island, Prince Edward Island, Maine, Oregon, Washington, or anyplace that grows good-quality potatoes. Idaho potatoes are considered by many to be better for French fries because they have a lower moisture content, but any good white potato will do. Waxy red potatoes are the only spuds that don't make great fries.

Or

> *3 to 4 medium sweet potatoes or*
> *2 to 3 medium boniato (Cuban sweet potatoes) or*
> *1 to 2 medium rutabagas or*
> *1 medium Caribbean yam or name*

Sweet potatoes, boniato, and rutabaga all have mellow flavors and good mealy textures that make great fries or chips. They can be used interchangeably or in place of regular white potatoes.

Celeriac, Hamburg parsley, and parsnip also make great fries and chips, but, at first, because not everyone is familiar with their more assertive flavors, I suggest you add them in with a large batch of potato fries and see if your guests like them.

Turnips, radishes, and beets don't make great fries because of their fairly high water content. They come out rather soggy and they don't crisp up. Carrots make okay fries but they don't seem to be best suited for this use.

How to Cut Them

There are two ways to cut fries and chips, either by hand or with a tool such as a mandoline or even a hand grater.

A mandoline is a restaurant tool of French origin that is a narrow, flat cutting surface with a blade and a slit hole in the middle. You scrape the vegetable across the blade and the chips fall out the bottom.

You can buy a good-quality plastic mandoline with three different blades at kitchen supply shops or from a catalogue such as Williams-Sonoma. They cost about $30. You can also buy a restaurant-quality stainless steel mandoline at specialty shops for over $125. An inexpensive hand-held grater is less versatile, but it can cut great thin potato chips and is available in most supermarkets for less than $5.

If you decide to cut the fries by hand, be sure to use a heavy, firmly constructed, stainless steel knife that is 6 to 8 inches long.

Peeling roots for fries is purely a matter of choice. It does not affect the cooking process. If you decide not to peel, be sure to scrub the roots thoroughly before cutting.

The most common cuts for root fries are:

Chips. Slice the roots across the grain into circles no more than ⅛ inch thick. If the root is really fat, like boniato, celery root, or an occasional oversized sweet or regular potato, cut them into lengthwise wedges and then into chips. A mandoline, hand-held grater, or even a food processor does a fast and even job of this.

Chunks. Chunks are really the equivalent of English chips. Use a sharp knife and cut the roots into wedges 1 inch long and ½ inch wide.

French fries. Using a sharp knife, cut the root lengthwise into slabs ¼ inch thick. Cut the slabs into ¼-inch-wide French fries.

Julienne. This is difficult to do with a knife unless you are experienced at handling a blade. Use a mandoline instead and cut the roots into long, ultrathin strips. The longer the julienne strips, the more chic the dish at New York restaurants.

Cooking Instructions

1. Wash and thoroughly dry the root pieces with cloth or paper toweling. They must be very dry.

2. Place the vegetable oil in a large, heavy pot with deep sides. Turn the heat to medium-high for about 3 minutes or until it reaches a temperature of 350°F to 375°F. If the oil is smoking, it is too hot and the roots will burn before they fry.

3. Toss one root into the oil to test. If it rises to the surface, sizzles, and begins to turn golden brown, it is ready. Add a handful of roots to just cover the surface of the hot oil. Do not crowd the pot.

4. Fry the roots until they are golden brown, stirring often, because agitation helps them brown better. Remove, drain, and keep warm. Continue frying until all roots are cooked.

5. Bring the oil back to 350°F to 375°F. Return all the roots to the pot and quickly fry for 1 minute to get them nice and crispy. Drain and serve immediately.

Flavoring and Savoring

Sprinkle the root fries with salt and maybe a little pepper. Dip them in ketchup, chili sauce, spicy ketchup, barbecue sauce, mustard, horseradish, or melted butter. You can also sprinkle them with malted English vinegar, cider, sherry, raspberry or other flavored vinegar, soy sauce, fish sauce, Worcestershire sauce, Pickapepper sauce, Louisiana hot sauce, Szechuan hot chili oil, Parmesan or Romano cheese, fresh minced parsley, cilantro or chervil, cayenne pepper, paprika, or anything else you like.

ROOTS NESTS AND BASKETS

Little nests or baskets made out of shredded root vegetables are very common in many Chinese restaurants. They usually are made from potatoes, but they can easily be made from other roots or roots and potatoes grated together. After they are fried and drained, they are usually filled with stir-fried shrimp or scallops in a light gravy.

To make them at home, you need to buy specially designed root fry basket makers. They are available at Chinese groceries or at specialty cookware shops. They are essentially two metal wire baskets, one about 4 inches in diameter, the other about 3 inches in diameter, each attached to long metal handles.

2 medium Idaho potatoes
2 medium sweet potatoes
1 quart vegetable oil

1. Wash and grate the white potatoes and the sweet potatoes. Place them in a medium mixing bowl and stir to combine them. Do not rinse the gratings or dry them with a towel. You need the moisture from the spuds to help them stick together.

2. Place the oil in a large, heavy, deep-sided pot and heat to 350°F to 375°F.

3. Place some of the grated potato mixture in the larger wire basket and press it gently up against the sides to form a little bowl of grated potatoes. Place the smaller basket inside, making sure that there is enough potato mixture spread evenly around the entire basket area. Secure the latch holding the two baskets together.

4. Place the potato basket into the hot oil and cook until golden brown. Watch it carefully because this will take only 2 to 3 minutes.

5. Drain the nests, remove from their baskets, and repeat. Keep all the baskets warm in the oven until ready to use.

Flavoring and Savoring
The various combinations of potatoes and other roots mentioned in the root fries section above are good for making root nests.

ONION RINGS

Onion rings were always the second choice at carhop, *American Graffiti*–type drive-in restaurants. People ordered onion rings when they wanted a break from French fries or if they just wanted to be different.

But onion rings can be a lot more versatile. Their batter can be seasoned to take on a new identity, or rings cut from a wider variety of onion flavors can give the dish a new interpretation. One of the most popular dishes at Lola's, a contemporary restaurant with Caribbean overtones in Manhattan, is zesty spiced onion rings.

>   *1 cup all-purpose flour*
>   *1 cup warm beer*
>   *1 egg*
>   *1 teaspoon salt*
>   *4 medium to large onions, any type*
>   *1 quart vegetable oil*

1. In a medium mixing bowl, blend the flour, beer, egg, and salt. Stir and let rest for 15 to 30 minutes.

2. Peel and slice the onions into ¼-inch-thick slices. Separate the slices into rings.

3. Heat the oil in a large, heavy, deep pot, deep-sided skillet, Dutch oven, or heavy wok. If you have a cooking thermometer, the temperature should read 375°F. If you don't, heat until just before the oil begins to smoke. Drop a bit of batter in. If it sinks to the bottom and slowly sizzles, the oil is too cold. If it fries madly and turns brown and burns, it is too hot. The tiny bit of batter should quickly rise to the surface and smoothly begin to turn a golden brown.

4. Drop a few onion rings into the batter and coat them thoroughly. Remove a few and let any excess batter drip off. Drop them into the oil to fill the pot or pan. Don't overcrowd. Fry them on one side until golden brown and flip them over. Remove from the oil,

drain on paper towels, and serve. Or keep them in a warm oven until all the rings are done.

Savoring and Flavoring

Onion rings are perfect just the way they are, sprinkled with a little salt. But try using red Spanish onions for a different color or sweet onions like Vidalia for a different flavor. You can even cut shallots in half, dip them in batter, and deep-fry as onion chunks.

Flavor the batter with chili powder, paprika, curry powder, or Chinese five-spice for variety.

TEMPURA AND FRITTO MISTO

Tempura and fritto misto are the Japanese and the Italian versions of a dish of batter-fried roots much like onion rings, only more extensive and elaborate.

> *2 cups all-purpose flour*
> *1½ cups water*
> *2 eggs*
> *1 sweet potato*
> *1 daikon radish*
> *1 to 2 small zucchini*
> *2 medium turnips*
> *2 to 3 medium sweet or red onions*
> *1 pound medium to medium-large shrimp, peeled and deveined*
> *1 quart vegetable oil for frying*

1. Make the batter by combining the flour, water, and eggs in a large mixing bowl. Stir to blend well. Let rest for 30 minutes.
2. Wash and peel the vegetables and slice into thin bite-sized pieces. Slice the onions into rings or wedges. Dry the vegetables and the shrimp on paper towels.

3. Heat the oil in a heavy, deep-sided pot to a temperature of 350°F to 360°F.

4. Dip an assortment of shrimp and vegetables into the batter and drop into the hot oil. Don't overcrowd the food. Fry until golden brown, about 1 to 2 minutes. Let the oil reheat in between batches so that it is good and hot. If the oil is not hot enough, the foods will absorb too much of the oil and be soggy and heavy with grease.

5. Drain and serve to your guests as soon as the ingredients are cooked. Tempura doesn't keep well.

Tempura is served with soy sauce that has been flavored with sesame seeds, grated ginger, minced scallions, or rice vinegar.

Fritto misto usually is served with nothing but a dusting of salt and pepper.

ROOT FRITTERS

There are many different interpretations of fritters. Doughnuts, beignets, and hush puppies are types of fritters. Fritters are essentially some type of dough or mush that is dropped in hot oil to cook.

Root fritters are composed of cooked and mashed root vegetables, bound with egg, seasoned with herbs and spices, enriched with bits of meat or fish, and deep-fried. You can put them in a paper bag and eat them out of hand like French fries or serve them as a side dish. Root fritters are a great way to use yesterday's mashed potatoes and other leftovers.

POTATO FRITTERS WITH SCALLIONS

2 to 3 medium white all-purpose potatoes
2 eggs
1½ cups finely chopped fresh green scallions
Salt and pepper to taste
1 quart vegetable oil for frying

1. Wash, peel, and coarsely chop the potatoes. Place them in a saucepan, cover with water, and boil until soft, about 15 to 20 minutes. Drain.

2. Place the potatoes in a large mixing bowl and mash. Add the eggs, scallions, salt, and pepper, and stir to blend well.

3. Place the oil in a heavy, deep pot and heat over medium-high heat until the oil is 350°F.

4. Form the fritters into tablespoon-sized shapes and drop them into the hot oil. Don't overcrowd the pot. Fry until golden brown. Remove and drain. Repeat. This makes about 10 to 15 fritters.

SWEET POTATO FRITTERS WITH HAM

2 to 3 medium sweet potatoes, about 1 pound
2 eggs
1 cup finely minced baked or boiled ham
½ teaspoon brown sugar (optional)
Pinch of mace or nutmeg
Salt and pepper to taste
1 quart vegetable oil

1. Peel and coarsely chop the sweet potatoes. Place in a pan of water and boil until soft, about 10 minutes.

2. Drain the potatoes and place in a large mixing bowl. Mash the potatoes and add the eggs, ham, sugar, mace or nutmeg, salt, and pepper. Stir to blend well.

3. Heat the oil in a heavy pot until 350°F.

4. Form the fritters into tablespoon-sized pieces and drop into the hot oil. Cook until golden brown. Drain and serve. Makes about 10 to 15 fritters.

CARIBBEAN ROOTS AND CLAM FRITTERS

1 pound Caribbean roots such as boniato, cassava,
*   malanga, taro, or yam*
2 eggs
1 cup chopped fresh or canned clams, drained
½ to 1 teaspoon curry powder, or to taste
Salt and pepper to taste
1 quart vegetable oil for frying

1. Peel, chop, and boil the roots in water to cover until tender, about 15 to 20 minutes. Drain.

2. Place the cooked roots in a large mixing bowl and mash. Add the eggs, clams, and seasonings.

3. Heat the oil in a heavy, deep-sided pot to 350°F.

4. Form the vegetable mixture into tablespoon-sized fritters and deep-fry until golden brown, about 2 to 3 minutes. Makes about 10 to 15 fritters.

In addition to white potatoes, sweet potatoes, and Caribbean roots, celeriac, parsnip, rutabaga, and carrots all make great fritters. Beets and turnips are good, too, but they should be blended with potatoes for better consistency.

EGG ROLLS AND WONTONS

Egg rolls and wontons are larger and smaller versions of the very same thing, namely a paper-thin sheet of dough that is wrapped around a filling of meats and vegetables, and is then deep-fried.

Usually egg rolls and wontons are stuffed with cabbage and a few other things, but there is no reason why they can't be stuffed with slivers of radish, jicama, sweet potato, turnip and carrot, and shreds of turnip greens, spiced with radish sprouts.

1 cup shredded jicama, daikon radish, sweet potato,
*   turnip, carrot, or a colorful mixture of them all*

1 cup radish sprouts or a mixture of bean and radish
    sprouts
1 cup finely minced turnip greens or a mixture of
    turnip greens and Chinese cabbage
¼ to ½ pound raw shrimp, shelled, deveined, and
    finely chopped
1 tablespoon vegetable oil
1 tablespoon each dry sherry and soy sauce
½ teaspoon sesame oil
1-pound package wonton or egg roll wrappers,
    found in the supermarket produce section or at a
    Chinese grocery
1 quart vegetable oil for frying

1. Sauté all the vegetables and the shrimp in the tablespoon of vegetable oil over medium-high heat for 3 to 5 minutes. Add the sherry, soy sauce, and sesame oil. Stir to blend well. Let cool.

2. Lay a wonton or egg roll wrapper on a working area in front of you. Place a teaspoon of the vegetable mixture in the middle of a wonton wrapper. Place a tablespoon of mixture on an egg roll wrapper.

3. Fold one edge of the wrapper over the mixture. Moisten the edges of the wrapper with water, fold the sides over the mixture, and roll the wrapper into a cylinder. An alternative method for smaller wontons is to draw the wrapper edges together like a purse and pinch to close.

4. Place the cooking oil in a heavy, deep-sided pot and heat to 350°F.

5. Place a few egg rolls or wontons in the hot oil and fry to a golden brown, about 3 to 5 minutes, turning occasionally.

6. Drain and serve with the following dipping sauces.

CHINESE MUSTARD SAUCE

Mix together 2 tablespoons dry mustard, 3 tablespoons dry sherry, and ½ cup beer or water in a small bowl.

SWEET AND SOUR SAUCE

Place ¾ cup water, ¼ cup vinegar, ⅓ cup brown sugar, 2 tablespoons soy sauce, and 1 tablespoon cornstarch in a small saucepan. Cook over medium-high heat for 5 minutes, stirring often until thick and syrupy.

FOUR

Soups and Chowders

Some of the most famous soups in the world are based on a wonderful variety of root vegetables. Vichyssoise has leeks and potatoes, minestrone has carrots, borscht has beets, and, of course, onion soup has onions galore. Roots have always felt right at home in a soup pot and, better yet, in a soup bowl.

This chapter is going to take a longer look at root soups and chowders and see where a larger variety of root vegetables can fit in and become new family favorites.

All the recipes in this chapter will yield 4 to 6 servings.

MY MOTHER'S POTATO SOUP

4 to 5 medium all-purpose Kennebec-type potatoes
1 medium onion
2 stalks celery or 1 small celery root
4 tablespoons unsalted butter
1 quart whole milk or half-and-half
Salt and freshly ground pepper to taste
2 tablespoons minced fresh scallion tops, chervil,
*   chives, parsley, dill, or a combination, for garnish*

1. Wash and peel the potatoes. Chop into ½-inch dice. Peel the onion and chop fine. Wash the celery and chop fine or peel the celery root and chop fine.

2. In a medium soup pot, melt the butter over medium heat for 2 minutes. Add the potatoes, onions, and celery or celery root. Sauté for 5 minutes, stirring often.

3. Add the milk and simmer over medium heat for 15 minutes. Remove 1 cup of the soup and purée in the blender or food proces-

sor. Return to the soup. This will help thicken the soup. Add salt and pepper to taste.

4. Ladle the soup into bowls and sprinkle with the minced herbs. Serve.

COLD BEET BORSCHT

3 to 4 medium-sized beets, about 1 pound
2 medium cucumbers, peeled and seeded
1 clove garlic, peeled
2 cups buttermilk or milk
2 cups sour cream or yogurt
Salt and freshly ground black pepper
2 scallions, finely chopped, white and green parts

1. Wash the beets and trim off any stems or woody parts. Place them in a pot, cover with water, and bring to a boil. Turn the heat to medium, cover the pot, and simmer for 30 to 40 minutes.

2. Drain and cool the beets in cold water. Peel and chop them and place in a food processor. Add the cucumbers, garlic, buttermilk, and sour cream to the food processor and process till the soup is smooth and creamy.

3. Add salt and pepper to taste, place in a large covered bowl, and chill in the refrigerator overnight or for at least 4 hours.

4. Ladle the soup into bowls, sprinkle with scallions, and serve.

MANY ONIONS SOUP

2 each medium-sized red, white, and yellow onions
5 shallots
3 cloves garlic
2 leeks
1 bunch scallions
4 tablespoons unsalted butter

> 1 teaspoon each sugar, salt, and freshly ground
>   black pepper
> 2 quarts rich beef stock or broth
> 1 loaf French bread
> ½ pound Swiss cheese

1. Peel the onions, shallots, and garlic. Chop fine. Carefully wash the leeks and scallions, and chop fine.

2. Melt the butter in a large soup pot over medium-high heat for 1 minute. Add the onions and scallions, stir, and reduce heat to medium. Cook the onions for 20 minutes, stirring often, until they begin to brown.

3. Add the sugar, salt, and pepper. Stir and brown for another 5 minutes. Add the broth, bring the soup to the boil, reduce the heat to medium-low, and cook, uncovered, for 30 minutes.

4. Slice and toast the French bread. Grate the cheese. Place each piece of bread in an individual soup bowl. Cover with grated cheese and ladle the soup over that. Serve.

JAMAICAN BOUILLABAISSE

> 1 malanga or boniato or 2 small taro
> 2 bottles clam juice
> 1 28-ounce can whole tomatoes or 4 medium fresh
>   tomatoes, peeled
> 2 cloves garlic, peeled and minced
> 1 teaspoon fresh minced ginger
> 1 hot chili pepper, minced, either Scotch Bonnet
>   or long red or green (optional)
> 1 pound firm-fleshed white fish such as cod or
>   grouper
> 1 cup chopped scallions

1. Wash and peel the malanga, boniato, or taro. Chop into bite-sized pieces. Place in a large soup pot, cover with water, and simmer for 10 minutes. Drain the water.

2. Add the clam juice, tomatoes, garlic, ginger, and chili pepper. Simmer for 10 minutes.

3. Slice the fish into bite-sized pieces. Gently place the fish into the pot and stir carefully to cover with soup. Add the scallions and cook for 5 to 7 minutes.

4. Ladle the soup and the fish chunks into large, flat soup bowls. Serve immediately or the fish will overcook and toughen.

HOT EASTERN EUROPEAN BORSCHT

½ to ¾ pound stewing beef
3 medium beets, peeled and shredded
1 medium onion, peeled and chopped
2 medium potatoes, peeled and diced
2 carrots, peeled and chopped
2 cups shredded cabbage
1 bay leaf
2 tablespoons fresh minced parsley
Salt and pepper to taste

1. Place the beef in a large soup pot and cover with 2 quarts water. Bring the soup to a boil, lower heat, cover the pot, and simmer for 1 hour.

2. Remove the meat from the pot and let cool. Shred the beef and return it to the pot. Add the vegetables to the pot and bring the soup to the boil. Add the bay leaf, parsley, salt, and pepper, and stir. Turn the heat to medium and simmer for 20 minutes or until the vegetables are tender.

3. Remove the bay leaf, check the seasonings, and serve.

CARROT BISQUE

4 slices thick-cut, hickory-smoked bacon
1½ pounds carrots, peeled and chopped
½ pound fresh mushrooms, chopped

1 bunch scallions, green and white parts, chopped
2 stalks celery, chopped
½ teaspoon dried thyme
1 bay leaf, whole
5 cups chicken stock, canned or homemade
1½ cups half-and-half or light cream
½ teaspoon each salt and freshly ground black
*   pepper*

1. In a large soup pot, sauté the bacon over medium heat till crisp. Add the carrots, mushrooms, the white part of the scallions, and the celery. Sauté the vegetables in the bacon drippings about 5 minutes.

2. Add the herbs, cover the pot, lower the heat, and let simmer another 5 minutes.

3. Add the chicken stock and simmer, covered, about 15 minutes. Remove the bay leaf and purée the soup in a blender or food processor.

4. Return the soup to the pot and add the cream or half-and-half. Add the salt and pepper. Warm the soup, stirring often, but do not let it boil. Serve the soup sprinkled with the reserved scallion tops.

SPRING CARROT SOUP

2 tablespoons unsalted butter
2 shallots or 1 small red onion, peeled and minced
1 small clove garlic, peeled and minced
2 medium carrots, peeled and chopped fine
½ cup fresh peas
½ cup chopped asparagus spears
6 cups rich chicken broth, canned or homemade
½ cup orzo pasta
1 tablespoon minced fresh parsley
Salt and pepper to taste

1. Melt the butter in a medium soup pot over medium heat. Add the shallots and garlic and sauté for 3 minutes. Add the carrots, peas, and asparagus and sauté another 2 minutes.

2. Add the chicken broth and the orzo pasta. Bring the pot to a boil, turn the heat to medium, and simmer for 10 minutes.

3. Add the parsley, salt, and pepper. Stir and serve hot.

AFRICAN CARROT AND PEANUT SOUP

> *3 tablespoons olive or other vegetable oil*
> *1 medium onion, peeled and chopped*
> *2 cloves garlic, peeled and chopped*
> *1 pound fresh carrots, scrubbed, peeled, and*
>   *chopped*
> *1 tablespoon curry powder*
> *¼ teaspoon cayenne pepper (optional)*
> *4 cups chicken broth, canned or homemade*
> *4 tablespoons crunchy peanut butter*
> *Freshly ground black pepper and salt to taste*
> *2 scallions, thinly sliced*
> *2 tablespoons unsalted roasted peanuts, crushed but*
>   *not powdered*

1. Heat the oil in a medium soup pot over medium heat. Add the onion and garlic and sauté for 4 minutes. Add the carrots, curry powder, and cayenne and sauté for another 2 minutes.

2. Add the chicken stock and bring to a boil. Reduce the heat to medium, cover, and simmer for 10 minutes.

3. Cool the soup slightly and whir in the food processor to form a creamy soup. Return the soup to the pot.

4. Turn the heat to medium, add the peanut butter to the pot, and stir to blend well. Add the black pepper and salt if you feel it is necessary.

5. Ladle the soup into individual soup bowls. Mix the scallions with the peanuts and sprinkle them on top.

COLD CREAM OF CARROT WITH DILL SOUP

1 tablespoon unsalted butter
2 shallots or 1 small red onion, peeled and minced
2 scallions, chopped
1 pound carrots, peeled and chopped
2 cups water
1 tablespoon minced fresh dill or chervil plus 4 to 6
  small fresh sprigs for garnish
2 cups half-and-half
Salt and pepper to taste

1. Melt the butter in a medium soup pot over medium heat. Add the shallots, scallions, and carrots. Sauté for 5 minutes.

2. Add the water and dill, bring to a boil, reduce the heat to medium, cover, and simmer for 5 minutes or until carrots are tender.

3. Let the carrots cool slightly. Add them to a food processor and whir to form a creamy soup. Add the half-and-half and place in the refrigerator overnight or for at least 4 hours.

4. Ladle the soup into bowls and decorate with the dill or chervil sprigs.

NEW ENGLAND CLAM CHOWDER

3 strips thick-cut slab bacon
1 large onion, peeled and chopped
2 medium all-purpose white Kennebec-type
  potatoes
1 parsnip
1 carrot
1 pint fresh minced clams
1 quart whole milk or half-and-half
Freshly ground pepper to taste

1. Fry the bacon in a medium soup pot until crispy brown. Remove, chop, and reserve.

2. Peel and dice the onion, potatoes, parsnip, and carrot. Add to

the hot fat and sauté for 5 minutes, stirring often.

3. Drain the clam juice from the clams and add it and the milk to the pot and simmer for 15 minutes or until vegetables are soft. Traditional clam chowder is not very thick, but if you prefer it thick, you can purée 1 cup of the soup at this time or simply mash the vegetables slightly with a potato masher.

4. Add the clams and pepper and cook for 2 minutes. Ladle the soup into bowls and sprinkle the chopped bacon on top.

CELERY SOUP PARISIAN

2 tablespoons butter or margarine
3 large shallots or 1 medium red onion, chopped fine
1 celery root, peeled and grated
1½ quarts rich beef broth or stock
Salt and pepper to taste
8 thin slices French bread, toasted
1 cup grated Swiss or Gruyère cheese

1. Place the butter in a medium-sized soup pot and turn the heat to medium-high. Add the shallots and sauté for 3 minutes. Add the celery root and sauté another 3 minutes.

2. Add the beef broth and salt and pepper to taste. Turn the heat to high and bring to a boil. Reduce the heat to medium and simmer the soup for 15 minutes.

3. Place a slice of toasted French bread in the bottom of a soup bowl. Sprinkle with cheese and cover with another slice of bread. Fill the bowl with soup and serve.

CELERIAC VICHYSSOISE

1 tablespoon butter or margarine
1 medium onion, peeled and chopped
1 large celery root, peeled and chopped
2 medium white potatoes, peeled and chopped

2 cups chicken stock
1 cup cream or half-and-half
Salt and pepper to taste
2 tablespoons minced fresh chives or parsley

1. Melt the butter in a soup pot over medium heat. Add the onion and sauté for 5 minutes, stirring often.

2. Add the celery root and potatoes and chicken stock. Bring to a boil, cover, reduce heat to medium, and simmer for 15 to 20 minutes or until tender.

3. Place the vegetables and stock in a food processor and blend until smooth and creamy. You may have to do this in batches.

4. Return the soup to the pot and add the cream or half-and-half. Add the salt and pepper. Turn the heat to medium-high and heat the soup thoroughly, but don't let it boil. The soup will begin to thicken.

5. To serve hot, ladle the soup into bowls and sprinkle with chives. Or chill it thoroughly in the refrigerator and then sprinkle with chives.

CORN AND PARSNIP CHOWDER

2 large parsnips
3 slices bacon, chopped into ½-inch pieces
1 medium onion, chopped
1 stalk celery, chopped
1 cup water
3 cups milk
2 cups fresh or frozen corn kernels
¼ to ½ teaspoon paprika
Salt and pepper to taste

1. Peel and chop the parsnips into ¼- to ½-inch chunks. Reserve.

2. Place the bacon slices in a soup pot and fry until crispy brown. Remove the bacon and drain on paper towels. Drain off all but 1 teaspoon of the drippings.

3. Add the parsnip, onion, and celery to the pot and cook over medium heat 5 minutes, stirring occasionally. Add the water and simmer 5 minutes.

4. Add the milk, corn, paprika, salt, and pepper and simmer 5 minutes.

5. Place 1 cup of the soup in a blender or food processor and whir to form a thick paste. Pour this back into the soup as a thickener.

6. Reheat the soup to hot but not boiling. Ladle into soup bowls and sprinkle the bacon bits on top.

WHITE BEAN AND VEGETABLE SOUP

2 tablespoons vegetable oil
1 medium yellow or white onion, peeled and
  chopped
1 Hamburg parsley root, peeled and chopped, or 1
  stalk celery
2 medium carrots, peeled and chopped
2 Yukon Gold potatoes, peeled and chopped
2 medium turnips, peeled and chopped
1 28-ounce can whole tomatoes
1 16-ounce can white beans, drained and rinsed
1 teaspoon each dried thyme and marjoram leaves
Salt and pepper to taste

1. Warm the vegetable oil in a medium soup pot. Add the onion, parsley root, carrots, potatoes, and turnips. Sauté for 5 minutes.

2. Add the tomatoes, beans, thyme, marjoram, salt, and pepper. Simmer over medium-low heat for 30 minutes. Serve.

PARSNIP SOUP WITH PORCINI MUSHROOMS

3 to 4 dried porcini mushrooms, about 2 ounces
1 tablespoon olive oil

1 medium onion, peeled and chopped fine
1 clove garlic, minced
1 pound parsnips, peeled and diced
1 cup chopped fresh button mushrooms
1 quart beef broth or stock
Salt and pepper to taste
2 tablespoons minced fresh parsley

1. Place the dried porcini mushrooms in a small bowl and cover with warm water. Let rest 15 to 20 minutes for the mushrooms to soak and get soft.

2. Remove the mushrooms and chop fine. Strain the remaining liquid through a fine mesh and save for the soup.

3. In a medium-sized soup pot, heat the oil over medium heat for 1 minute. Add the onion, garlic, parsnips, and fresh mushrooms. Sauté for 3 to 5 minutes.

4. Add the porcini mushrooms, the reserved mushroom water, the beef stock, salt, pepper, and parsley. Bring to a boil, reduce heat to low, and simmer for 15 minutes.

CREAM OF RUTABAGA SOUP

2 tablespoons butter or margarine
1 medium onion, peeled and chopped fine
1 clove garlic, peeled and minced
1 large rutabaga, peeled and chopped, about 2 cups
1½ cups chicken stock or broth
1 cup light cream or half-and-half
1 tablespoon fresh minced parsley
Salt and pepper to taste

1. In a medium soup pot, melt the butter over medium heat for 1 minute. Add the onion and garlic and sauté for 3 minutes.

2. Add the rutabaga and stock. Bring the pot to the boil, cover, and reduce heat to low. Simmer for 15 minutes or until the rutabaga is tender.

3. Let the rutabaga cool slightly and place the soup in a food processor and whir to form a smooth soup.

4. Return the soup to the pot and add the cream, parsley, and salt and pepper. Heat the soup over low heat for 10 minutes but do not let it boil.

RUTABAGA CHOWDER WITH SMOKED SAUSAGE

1 tablespoon vegetable oil
1 medium onion, chopped fine
½ pound smoked sausage, kielbasy, or frankfurters
1 large rutabaga, peeled and chopped in ½-inch dice
¼ cup water
2 tablespoons all-purpose flour
1 quart milk
Salt and pepper to taste

1. In a medium-sized soup pot, warm the oil over medium heat for 1 minute. Add the onion, sausage, and rutabaga. Sauté for 3 to 5 minutes.

2. Add the water, cover the pot, and cook for 10 minutes or until rutabaga is soft.

3. Mix the flour with ¼ cup of the milk and pour over the rutabaga. Stir to blend well. Add the remaining milk and heat through. As the chowder thickens, stir well to make a creamy soup.

4. Season with salt and pepper and serve.

CREAM OF TURNIP SOUP WITH SCALLIONS

4 medium turnips, washed and peeled
4 large scallions
2 tablespoons butter
2 cups chicken broth or stock
1 cup light or heavy cream
Pinch of nutmeg
Salt and freshly ground black pepper to taste

1. Chop the turnips coarsely. Remove the white bulbs from the green stems of the scallions. Coarsely chop the white bulbs and finely mince the green tops.

2. Melt the butter in a soup pot over medium heat. Add the turnips and scallion bulbs. Sauté for 2 minutes. Add the chicken stock and simmer for 15 minutes.

3. Purée the mixture in a food processor to form a creamy soup. Return the soup to the pot and add the cream, nutmeg, salt, and pepper. Cook over medium heat 5 minutes.

4. Serve in soup bowls and sprinkle the chopped green stems of the scallions on top as garnish.

SUMMER TURNIP SOUP WITH TOMATOES AND YELLOW CORN

> 1 tablespoon olive or other vegetable oil
> 1 small onion, peeled and minced
> 3 medium turnips
> 3 medium tomatoes
> 2 ears yellow corn
> 2 tablespoons minced fresh herbs such as parsley,
>   basil, thyme, savory, or chervil
> 1 quart beef broth or stock
> ½ pound lean ground beef (optional)
> Salt and pepper to taste

1. Warm the oil in a soup pot over medium heat for 1 minute. Add the onion and sauté for 2 minutes.

2. Peel and chop the turnips into ¼- to ½-inch dice. Peel and chop the tomatoes to a similar size. Cut the corn kernels from the corn.

3. Add the turnips, tomatoes, and corn to the pot. Stir. Add the fresh herbs and beef broth. Simmer the soup for 10 minutes.

4. Form the ground beef into ½-teaspoon-sized meatballs and add them to the soup. Simmer for 5 minutes. Add the salt and pepper.

UNDERGROUND SOUP

2 tablespoons olive oil
1 large onion, chopped fine
2 pounds beef for stew
2 quarts beef stock or water
1 bay leaf
1 teaspoon dried thyme
1 medium rutabaga, peeled and cut into ½-inch dice
2 carrots, peeled and cut into ½-inch circles
2 turnips, peeled and diced
1 small celeriac, peeled and diced
2 small parsnips, peeled and sliced into thin circles
Salt and pepper to taste

1. Warm the olive oil over medium heat for 1 minute. Add the onion and beef and sauté for 2 minutes. Add the stock or water, bring to a boil, reduce the heat to medium-low, and simmer (do not let it boil again) for 2 hours, partially covered. Skim the fat from the liquid and discard.

2. Add the bay leaf and thyme, rutabaga, carrots, celeriac, and parsnips. Simmer for 20 minutes or until vegetables are tender. Season with salt and pepper and serve.

MINESTRONE DELLA TERRA

3 tablespoons olive oil
1 medium onion, chopped fine
2 cloves garlic, minced
1 small celeriac, peeled and diced
1 large or 2 small carrots, diced
2 cups escarole, finely chopped
4 cups chicken or beef stock or water
2 cups chopped tomatoes, fresh or canned
1 16-ounce can white beans
½ cup ditali pasta, boiled until tender and drained
1 teaspoon each oregano and basil

2 bay leaves
Salt and pepper to taste
Grated Romano or Parmesan cheese

1. In a large soup pot, sauté the onion, garlic, celeriac, carrots, and escarole in the olive oil over medium-high heat for 3 minutes.

2. Add the beef stock and tomatoes and simmer for 20 minutes. Add the beans, pasta, oregano, basil, bay leaves, salt, and pepper. Simmer for 10 minutes.

3. Serve in wide soup bowls and pass the grated cheese.

CHINESE ROOTS AND CHICKEN SOUP

2 ounces dried Chinese mushrooms
1 3-pound chicken
1 leek, washed and sliced
1 small celeriac, peeled and diced
2 carrots, peeled and diced
2 cloves garlic, minced
1 tablespoon minced fresh ginger
6 uncooked flat wonton noodles
2 tablespoons soy sauce
1 tablespoon sesame oil
2 scallions, minced, green and white parts

1. Place the mushrooms in a small mixing bowl and cover with very hot water. Let mushrooms soak for 15 minutes. Trim off the woody stems and slice the caps. Reserve.

2. Place the chicken in a 4-quart soup pot. Cover with water and bring to a boil. Reduce the heat to medium-low and simmer for 45 minutes. Skim the scum as it rises to the top.

3. Remove the chicken from the soup. Debone the chicken and discard the fat and bones. Tear the chicken into bite-sized pieces.

4. Put the mushrooms, leek, celeriac, carrots, garlic, and ginger in the chicken broth. Simmer over medium-high heat for 15 minutes.

5. Slice the wonton skins into thin strips and add to the soup. Add

the chicken to the soup. Add the soy sauce, sesame oil, and scallions to the soup. Heat for 3 minutes and serve.

CREAM OF CURRIED ROOTS SOUP

3 tablespoons vegetable oil
1 clove garlic, minced
1 medium onion, chopped
1 tablespoon curry powder
1 small celeriac, peeled and chopped
2 carrots, peeled and chopped
2 turnips, peeled and chopped
1 medium white all-purpose potato
Salt and pepper to taste
2 cups half-and-half

1. In a large soup pot, heat the oil over medium-high heat for 1 minute. Add the garlic and onion and sauté for 3 minutes. Add the curry powder and the celeriac, carrots, turnips, and potato and sauté for 1 minute.

2. Add enough water to cover the vegetables, cover the pot, and simmer for 15 to 20 minutes. Cool slightly and purée in a food processor or mash with a potato masher.

3. Return the smooth soup to the pot and add the salt and pepper to taste.

4. Add the half-and-half and heat through but do not boil. Reduce the heat to medium-low and cook for 20 minutes. Let soup rest for 20 minutes for flavors to develop. Reheat but do not boil.

SPLIT PEA SOUP WITH HAM

2 tablespoons olive oil
1 medium onion, peeled and chopped fine
2 carrots, peeled and chopped, or 1 cup chopped
    rutabaga

2 medium potatoes, peeled and chopped
1 ham bone or smoked ham hock
1 pound green or yellow split peas
Salt and pepper to taste

1. Place the oil in a medium soup pot. Heat over medium heat for 1 minute. Add the onion and sauté for 2 minutes.

2. Add the carrots, potatoes, ham bone, and peas. Cover with 1 quart water or chicken broth. Bring to a boil, reduce heat to medium-low, and simmer for 30 minutes. Add more water if necessary.

3. Remove the ham bone or hock and trim off any meat. Return meat to the soup and discard bone. Add salt and pepper as necessary. Serve.

LONG ISLAND CLAM CHOWDER

3 tablespoons olive oil or other vegetable oil
1 medium red onion, peeled and diced
1 small celery or parsley root or 2 stalks celery, diced
1 carrot, peeled and diced
1 leek, cleaned and diced
3 cloves garlic, peeled and minced
¼ to ½ cup fresh minced parsley
2 white Long Island potatoes, peeled and diced
1 cup clam juice, water, or white wine
1 16-ounce can crushed tomatoes
½ teaspoon each dried basil, oregano, thyme, salt,
    and pepper
1 pint chopped fresh clams

1. In a medium soup pot, heat the oil over medium heat for 1 minute. Add the onion, celery root, carrot, leek, garlic, parsley, and potatoes. Cook and stir for 5 minutes.

2. Add the clam juice, tomatoes, and seasonings. Simmer for 15 minutes or until vegetables are soft. Add the clams, simmer over low heat for 5 minutes, and serve.

THAI-STYLE VEGETABLE SOUP WITH DAIKON

1 tablespoon vegetable oil
2 shallots, peeled and thinly sliced
3 cloves garlic, peeled and thinly sliced
1 teaspoon minced fresh ginger
5 cups chicken broth or stock
2 cups julienne-sliced daikon radish
1 teaspoon Thai fish sauce or light soy sauce
1 long red chili pepper, minced
½ cup thinly sliced turnip greens
½ cup minced fresh scallions
1 tablespoon fresh lime juice

1. Heat the oil in a medium soup pot over medium heat for 1 minute. Add the shallots, garlic, and fresh ginger. Cook for 1 minute, stirring often.

2. Add the chicken broth, daikon radish, fish sauce, and chili pepper. Simmer over medium heat for 15 minutes. Add turnip greens and scallions and simmer 10 minutes.

3. Add lime juice and serve.

ITALIAN TURNIP GREENS SOUP
WITH BOW TIE PASTA

1 cup bow tie pasta
2 tablespoons olive oil
2 shallots, peeled and chopped fine
1 bunch turnip greens, washed and chopped into
*   fine threads, about 2 cups*
4 cups chicken broth or stock
Salt and pepper to taste
½ cup grated Parmesan cheese

1. Boil the bow tie pasta in water until al dente. Drain and reserve.

2. Heat the oil in a medium soup pot for 1 minute. Add the

shallots and cook for 1 minute. Add the turnip greens and chicken stock. Simmer for 5 minutes.

3. Add the bow tie pasta and simmer for 3 minutes. Season with salt and pepper.

4. Ladle the soup into bowls and sprinkle with grated Parmesan.

CHEDDAR CHEESE AND ROOT SOUP

3 tablespoons unsalted butter or vegetable oil
1 leek, carefully washed and chopped
2 parsnips, peeled and chopped
1 medium turnip, peeled and chopped
1 medium white potato, peeled and chopped
2 cups chicken broth or stock
2 tablespoons unbleached whole wheat or all-pur-
pose flour
2 cups shredded aged Cheddar, Caerphilly, or other
British cheese
2 cups whole milk or half-and-half
Salt and pepper to taste

1. Melt 1 tablespoon of the butter in a medium soup pot over medium heat for 1 minute. Add the leek, parsnips, turnip, and potato and cook for 5 minutes, stirring often.

2. Add the chicken broth and simmer for 15 minutes or until the vegetables are tender.

3. Place the remaining butter and the flour together in a small bowl. Using a fork, mix the two together to form a dry paste. Add this to the soup and stir. It will begin to thicken.

4. Add the cheese and stir until the cheese melts. Add the milk, salt, and pepper and simmer the soup for 10 minutes, but do not boil.

MEXICAN SHRIMP SOUP WITH JICAMA

5 cups water
1 pound medium shrimp in their shells
2 tablespoons olive oil
2 cloves garlic, peeled and minced
1 jalapeño, serrano, or long green chili pepper,
    chopped fine
1 jicama, peeled and cut into ¼- to ½-inch dice
Salt and pepper to taste
¼ cup fresh minced cilantro or parsley

1. Place the water in a medium soup pot and bring to the boil. Add
the shrimp, return to the boil and turn off the heat. Let the shrimp
sit in the hot water for 3 minutes.

2. Remove shrimp from the water. Peel the shrimp and return the
peels to the water. Simmer over medium heat, uncovered, for 15
minutes. Strain the shrimp stock by pouring it through a colander
lined with cheesecloth. Reserve.

3. In a medium soup pot, heat the oil over medium heat 1 minute.
Add the garlic, jalapeño pepper, and jicama and sauté for 3 minutes.
Add the shrimp stock, salt, and pepper and cook for 5 minutes.

4. Add the shrimp pieces and the cilantro. Heat for 1 minute and
serve.

HOT PEPPER SWEET POTATO CHOWDER

2 pounds sweet potatoes
2 tablespoons unsalted butter or vegetable oil
1 medium red onion, peeled and chopped fine
2 cloves garlic, peeled and minced
1 jalapeño, serrano, or long green chili pepper,
    chopped fine
1 large sweet red bell pepper, seeded and chopped
1 quart chicken stock or broth
¼ teaspoon ground allspice

Salt and pepper to taste
1 cup whole milk or half-and-half
½ cup minced scallions, tops included, for garnish

1. Peel and chop the sweet potatoes. Place in a pot, cover with water, and simmer for 20 minutes. Drain and mash.

2. In a medium pot, heat the butter or oil over medium heat for 1 minute. Add the onion, garlic, hot pepper, and sweet pepper. Cook, stirring often, for 5 minutes.

3. Add the sweet potatoes, chicken stock, allspice, salt, and pepper. Stir and simmer over medium heat for 15 minutes.

4. Add the milk and heat but do not boil. Ladle the soup into bowls and sprinkle with scallion garnish.

FIVE

Salads

Too often when people think of salad they conjure up a picture of green lettuce leaves covered with a dressing. But let your mind wander through a typical salad bar and what do you see? Carrots and radishes immediately come to mind. It's not uncommon to find pickled beets there, too, and certainly some type of potato salad.

So, you see, root vegetables have long been a major part of any well-prepared salad. This chapter is going to add a lot of new ideas for roots salads that could easily liven up any salad bar.

All of the recipes in this chapter will yield 4 to 6 servings.

WARM ROOTS SALAD VINAIGRETTE

> *2 small beets*
> *1 small celeriac, peeled and diced*
> *2 small turnips, peeled and diced*
> *1 parsnip, peeled and diced*
> *1 shallot, minced*
> *2 tablespoons balsamic vinegar*
> *6 tablespoons olive oil*
> *¼ teaspoon dried thyme leaves*
> *¼ cup minced fresh parsley*
> *Salt and pepper to taste*

1. Boil the beets separately in a pan of water. Drain, cool, and cut into small dice. Place the celeriac, turnips, and parsnip in a pan of water and boil until tender, about 8 minutes. Drain and keep warm.

2. In a medium mixing bowl, combine the shallot, balsamic vinegar, olive oil, thyme, parsley, salt, and pepper. Whisk to form a creamy dressing.

3. Combine the beets with the other vegetables. Pour the vinaigrette over and toss. Serve immediately or keep warm by placing in the oven on low heat or microwave at the last moment.

SCANDINAVIAN ROOTS POTATO SALAD

3 medium red waxy potatoes
1 small rutabaga, quartered
3 medium turnips
½ pound cervelat sausages, knockwurst, or wieners
½ cup sour cream
½ cup yogurt
1 tablespoon fresh minced or 1 teaspoon dried dill
*   weed*
1 tablespoon spicy brown mustard
1 tablespoon prepared horseradish
Salt and pepper to taste

1. Wash and peel the potatoes, rutabaga, and turnips. Place them in a large pot of water, bring to a boil, and cook for 20 minutes or until the roots are tender-crisp.

2. Drain and cool. Peel and chop all the roots into ½-inch dice or ½-inch slices.

3. Place the sausages in simmering water for 3 minutes, just till they heat through. Drain and cool. Slice them into ¼-inch circles.

4. In a large mixing bowl, combine the sour cream, yogurt, dill, mustard, horseradish, salt, and pepper. Stir to blend well. Add the roots and sausages and stir to blend well. Chill for 1 hour and serve.

MEXICAN SHRIMP AND JICAMA SALAD

¾ pound fresh shrimp, shells on
3 ears fresh or frozen corn
1 jicama, peeled and diced
1 red sweet bell pepper, seeded and diced

3 tablespoons sherry wine vinegar or red wine
vinegar
½ cup olive oil
Salt and pepper to taste
4 to 6 large lettuce leaves

1. Bring 1 quart of water to the boil, add the shrimp, return to the boil, turn off heat, and let shrimp rest for 5 minutes. Drain and peel the shrimp. Reserve.

2. Husk the fresh corn. Boil either the fresh or frozen corn in a large pot of boiling water for 10 minutes. Remove and cool. Cut the corn kernels from the cobs. Reserve.

3. Place the shrimp, corn, jicama, and bell pepper in a medium mixing bowl. Add the sherry, olive oil, salt, and pepper. Stir to blend well. Serve mounded on lettuce leaves.

WARM BEETS IN SOUR CREAM
AND HORSERADISH

2 pounds fresh whole beets, tops removed
Salt and pepper to taste
½ cup sour cream or yogurt
1½ tablespoons prepared horseradish
2 scallions, white parts only

1. Boil the whole beets in water to cover in a covered pot 20 to 30 minutes, or until tender to the fork. Drain and peel.

2. Dice the still-warm beets. Sprinkle them with the salt and pepper. Blend the beets with the sour cream or yogurt and horseradish. Serve sprinkled with the chopped white scallions.

BEETS AND FRESH MOZZARELLA CHEESE SALAD

> *4 medium- to large-sized beets*
> *8 ounces fresh or packaged mozzarella cheese*
> *1 tablespoon red wine vinegar*
> *1 teaspoon Dijon mustard*
> *3 tablespoons olive oil*
> *Salt and pepper to taste*
> *¼ cup fresh minced basil leaves*

1. Trim the leaves off the beets and wash. Place the beets in a large pot with water to cover and boil until tender, about 20 to 30 minutes. Drain and cool.

2. Slice the beets and mozzarella paper-thin. Place the beets and cheese on a platter in alternating red and white layers.

3. Mix the wine vinegar with the Dijon mustard to form a creamy paste. Add the olive oil, salt, and pepper, and whisk to form a creamy dressing.

4. Sprinkle the minced basil over the beets and cheese. Drizzle the dressing over that.

SALAD LORETTE

> *4 large fresh heads of mâche, a.k.a. lamb's-lettuce or*
> *corn salad*
> *4 medium beets*
> *2 tablespoons tarragon white wine vinegar*
> *6 tablespoons olive oil*
> *Salt and black pepper to taste*
> *¾ cup finely chopped celery*
> *1 tablespoon tiny capers*

1. Wash and separate the heads of mâche. Drain and dry with paper towels.

2. Boil the beets in water to cover until tender-crisp, about 30 minutes. Drain and peel when cool enough to handle. Cut the beets in half and then into thin slices.

3. Whisk the vinegar, olive oil, salt, and pepper together to form a creamy dressing.

4. Toss the mâche with the beets, the celery, and the salad dressing to coat well. Place the mixture on individual salad plates and sprinkle with capers.

BEETS WITH WILD RICE AND HARD-COOKED EGGS

> *1 cup wild rice or wild rice blend*
> *4 cups water*
> *4 medium beets*
> *½ cup crumbly blue cheese*
> *1 cup unflavored yogurt*
> *4 hard-boiled eggs, peeled and thinly sliced*

1. Place the wild rice and water in a 2-quart saucepan. Bring to the boil, cover, reduce heat to medium-low, and simmer for 30 to 40 minutes. Turn off the heat and let rest 10 minutes. Stir with a fork to fluff and let cool to room temperature.

2. Boil the beets in water to cover until tender, about 30 minutes. Drain, and when cool enough to handle, peel. Chop the beets into ¼- to ½-inch dice.

3. Mash the blue cheese into the yogurt to form a creamy dressing or purée in a food processor.

4. Mound the wild rice on four individual salad plates. Using a spoon, create a "lake" or indentation in the center of each wild rice pile. Line the lake with egg slices and fill the indentation with diced beets. Spoon a portion of yogurt dressing on top of the beets and serve.

BEETS WITH SOUR CREAM AND DILL

3 to 4 medium beets, about 1 pound
2 medium cucumbers
1 cup sour cream
1 tablespoon fresh minced dill plus
4 to 6 small sprigs fresh dill
Salt and pepper to taste

1. Wash and trim the beets. Place them in a pot and cover with water. Bring the pot to a boil, turn the heat to medium, and simmer for 35 to 40 minutes.

2. Drain and peel the beets. Quarter the beets and slice the quarters as thin as possible.

3. Peel the cucumbers and slice them lengthwise into quarters. Scrape out the seeds and slice the cucumbers as thin as possible.

4. In a medium bowl, blend the beets with the sour cream, dill, salt, and pepper. Place equal portions of cucumbers on small salad plates, making a bed for the beets. Spoon the beets in a pile on the cucumbers, decorate with a sprig of dill, and serve.

TABOULE BEET SALAD

1 cup bulgur wheat for taboule
3 medium beets, washed and trimmed
1 small onion, peeled and minced
1 small clove garlic, peeled and minced
½ cup minced fresh parsley
1 cup low-fat plain yogurt
½ teaspoon ground cumin
2 tablespoons minced fresh mint, if available

1. Place taboule in a medium bowl. Pour 1½ cups cold water over, stir, and let stand for 30 minutes. Stir to separate the grains and let rest.

2. Place the beets in a pot and cover with water. Bring the pot to

a boil, turn the heat to medium, and simmer for 35 to 40 minutes. Drain and peel.

3. Chop the beets fine and place in the bowl with the taboule. Add the onion, garlic, parsley, yogurt, cumin, and mint. Stir to blend well.

BEETS AND BEET GREENS WITH BACON VINAIGRETTE

1 pound beet greens
2 medium whole beets
2 slices bacon
2 teaspoons apple cider vinegar
1 teaspoon Dijon mustard
2 tablespoons olive oil
Freshly ground black pepper to taste
1 shallot or small red onion, finely minced

1. Carefully wash the beet greens by plunging them into a large pail of water. Rinse, change the water, and wash the greens again to free them of any dirt or grit. Drain and chop into ½-inch ribbons.

2. Wash and peel the whole beets and slice into slivers. Cut the bacon into slices, too.

3. Sauté the bacon in a large pot until crispy. Remove the bacon with a slotted spoon and drain. Pour off all but 1 tablespoon of the bacon drippings and discard.

4. Put the beets and beet greens in the pot and stir. Add 1 cup of water, cover, and simmer over medium-high heat for 10 minutes. Drain and keep warm.

5. Pour the vinegar into a large mixing bowl. Add the mustard and whisk to form a creamy paste. Add the olive oil and black pepper and whisk to form a creamy dressing. Add the beets and beet greens to the dressing and toss.

6. Place a pile of beets and beet greens on individual salad plates. Sprinkle with the bacon bits and the minced shallot.

MEXICAN CARROT SLAW

>   *3 large carrots, washed and peeled*
>   *¼ head fresh green cabbage*
>   *2 jalapeño peppers*
>   *1 tablespoon chopped fresh cilantro*
>   *1 tablespoon fresh lime juice*
>   *2 tablespoons olive or vegetable oil*
>   *½ teaspoon chili powder*

1. Finely shred the carrots and cabbage and place them in a large mixing bowl. Mince the jalapeño peppers and add them to the carrot/cabbage. Remove the seeds if you don't want the salad to be too hot.

2. Mince the cilantro and place it in a small mixing bowl. Add the lime juice, olive oil, and chili powder. Stir to form a smooth dressing.

3. Pour the dressing over the slaw and stir. Let rest 15 minutes and serve.

CAJUN CELERIAC RÉMOULADE

>   *2 medium celeriacs*
>   *1 cup mayonnaise*
>   *1 tablespoon lemon juice*
>   *2 tablespoons Creole or spicy brown mustard*
>   *2 green onions, chopped fine*
>   *1 stalk celery, minced*
>   *¼ teaspoon cayenne pepper*
>   *2 tablespoons minced fresh parsley*
>   *1 teaspoon paprika*
>   *1 teaspoon Worcestershire sauce*
>   *Salt and pepper to taste*
>   *4 to 6 large lettuce leaves, washed and dried*

1. Wash and peel the celeriacs. Grate them by hand or with a food processor. Place in a medium saucepan and cover with water. Bring

the water to the boil, reduce the heat to medium, and simmer the celeriac for 5 minutes until tender-crisp. Drain and rinse with cold water.

2. Place the mayonnaise and the rest of the ingredients except the lettuce in a large mixing bowl. Stir to make a creamy dressing. Mix the dressing with the celeriac and stir to blend well. Let rest 15 minutes.

3. Place lettuce leaves on individual salad plates. Mound a portion of celeriac on each and serve.

CARROT-APPLE-RAISIN SALAD

1 large red, green, or yellow apple
2 medium carrots, washed and peeled
2 tablespoons raisins
½ cup mayonnaise
1 teaspoon lemon juice

1. Core and chop the apple into ½-inch dice. Place in a medium mixing bowl. Grate the carrots and add to the apple.

2. Add the raisins, mayonnaise, and lemon juice. Mix well.

CELERIAC WITH GRUYERE CHEESE AND WALNUT VINAIGRETTE

2 medium celeriacs
6 ounces Gruyère or Swiss cheese
½ cup chopped walnuts
1 teaspoon Dijon mustard
2 tablespoons white wine vinegar
2 tablespoons walnut oil
4 tablespoons olive or other vegetable oil
Salt and pepper to taste
Lettuce leaves for garnish

1. Wash, trim, and grate the celeriacs. Place in a medium saucepan and cover with water. Bring the water to the boil, reduce the heat to medium, and simmer 5 minutes or until tender-crisp. Drain and rinse in cold water. Place in a large mixing bowl.

2. Grate the cheese with the same-size grater as the celeriac. You want the celeriac and cheese to look similar. Toss the cheese and celeriac together. Add the walnuts and toss again.

3. In a separate mixing bowl, stir the mustard and vinegar together to form a creamy paste. Add the walnut oil and whisk. Add the olive or vegetable oil and whisk to form a creamy dressing. Add salt and pepper to taste.

4. Add the celeriac-and-cheese mixture to the dressing and toss to coat. Place lettuce leaves on individual salad plates. Mound a portion of salad on each plate and serve.

SALAD NIÇOISE CELERIAC

> *2 medium celeriacs*
> *½ pound slender young green beans*
> *1 large or 2 medium ripe tomatoes*
> *2 hard-boiled eggs*
> *1 large or 2 medium green bell peppers*
> *1 6-ounce can solid pack white tuna fish, drained*
> *2 tablespoons lemon juice*
> *6 tablespoons fruity olive oil*
> *1 tablespoon chopped fresh herbs, either chives, tar-*
>   *ragon, basil, parsley, or a combination*
> *Salt and pepper to taste*
> *6 to 8 anchovy fillets (optional)*
> *¾ cup mixed black and green olives (optional)*

1. Peel the celeriacs and place in a large saucepan. Add water to cover and boil for 15 to 20 minutes or until tender-crisp. Drain and rinse in cold water. Slice into rounds, wedges, or strips.

2. Steam the green beans until tender-crisp, drain, and plunge into

cold water. Drain and reserve. Slice the tomatoes. Peel the eggs and slice. Slice the pepper.

3. Arrange the celeriac, green beans, tomatoes, eggs, peppers, and tuna fish on a large platter.

4. Make the dressing by whisking the lemon juice with the olive oil. Add the herbs, salt, and pepper, and pour over the arranged vegetables. Lay the anchovy fillets on top and scatter the olives over all. Serve with French bread and butter for lunch.

WARM GERMAN RUTABAGA SALAD

2 medium rutabagas
2 slices bacon
1 small red onion, chopped fine
¼ cup red wine or apple cider vinegar
¼ cup water
½ teaspoon sugar
Salt and pepper to taste
Pinch of mace (optional)
¼ cup minced chives or parsley

1. Peel the rutabagas and slice them into quarters. Place in a saucepan, cover with water, and boil until tender, about 20 to 25 minutes. Drain and slice into thin pieces.

2. In a large skillet or Dutch oven, fry the bacon until crisp. Remove bacon and drain. Add the onion to the drippings and fry for 3 minutes. Add the rutabaga and stir to coat with oil.

3. Add the vinegar, water, sugar, salt and pepper, and mace and cook over medium-high heat for 3 minutes, stirring frequently.

4. Spoon the salad into a large serving bowl, sprinkle with chives or parsley, and serve warm.

TURNIP SALAD WITH
GREEN BEANS VINAIGRETTE

2 medium turnips
½ pound slender green beans
2 tablespoons tarragon white wine vinegar
1 teaspoon coarse-grained brown mustard
6 tablespoons olive oil
Salt and pepper to taste
1 tablespoon fresh minced parsley, basil, or tarragon
  or a combination

1. Peel the turnips and cut into julienne strips. Trim the ends and stems off the green beans and cut them into lengths the same size as the turnips.

2. Place the turnips and green beans in a pot of boiling water and cook for 5 minutes. Drain and plunge into a pot of cold water. Drain.

3. In a large mixing bowl, blend the wine vinegar with the mustard and stir to form a creamy paste. Add the olive oil and whisk to form a creamy dressing. Add the salt, pepper, and herbs. Stir to blend well. Add the turnips and beans to the dressing and toss to coat well.

TURNIP AND WATERCRESS SALAD
WITH BLUE CHEESE

3 medium turnips, washed and peeled
1 large bunch watercress
¾ cup crumbly blue cheese
1 cup buttermilk

1. Chop the turnips into quarters and slice each quarter into thin pieces. Place them in a saucepan, cover with water, and simmer for 5 to 8 minutes. Drain and cool.

2. Wash the watercress and remove any damaged branches or discolored leaves. Create watercress "nests" on four individual salad

plates. Create a mound of turnip slices in the middle of each "nest."

3. Blend half the blue cheese with the buttermilk in a food processor to form a creamy sauce. Drizzle the sauce over the salads and garnish with the rest of the crumbly cheese.

RED AND GOLDEN BEET SALAD ON A BED OF BEET GREENS

4 red beets with tops
4 golden beets with tops
2 tablespoons orange juice
1 teaspoon Dijon mustard
Salt and pepper to taste
6 tablespoons olive oil
2 tablespoons toasted sesame seeds (optional)

1. Cut the beet greens from the beets and wash carefully. Trim off any stems. Chop the beet greens and steam them for 5 minutes, just till they are wilted and tender. Rinse in cold water and drain.

2. Cook the whole beets separately in different pots of boiling water, about 20 minutes, until they are tender but not mushy. Drain and cool. Peel the beets.

3. Cut the beets into thin slices. Place a layer of beet greens on individual salad plates. Place the beets on top in alternating layers of red and orange.

4. In a separate bowl, whisk together the orange juice, mustard, salt, and pepper. Whisk in the oil to form a creamy dressing. Pour the dressing over the beets and sprinkle with the sesame seeds if you wish.

MULTICOLORED INTERNATIONAL POTATO SALAD

> 1 medium-large purple Peruvian potato
> 2 small yellow Finnish potatoes
> 1 small sweet potato
> 1 small boniato (Cuban white sweet potato)
> 2 hard-cooked eggs
> ½ cup diced celery
> ½ cup chopped scallions, with tops
> 1 teaspoon sugar
> 2 tablespoons cider vinegar or your favorite vinegar
> 1 cup mayonnaise
> Salt and pepper to taste

1. Wash the potatoes and cook them in boiling water until tender, about 20 minutes. Drain and cool.

2. Peel the potatoes and hard-cooked eggs. Dice and place in a medium mixing bowl. Add the celery, scallions, sugar, vinegar, mayonnaise, salt, and pepper. Stir to blend well. Feel free to add a little more mayonnaise, sour cream, or yogurt if you like a creamier texture.

ASIAN GINGERED COLE SLAW

> 2 cups finely shredded Chinese cabbage
> 1 cup grated daikon radish
> 1 cup grated carrot
> 1 teaspoon minced fresh ginger
> ⅓ cup olive or vegetable oil
> 1 tablespoon Chinese or white wine vinegar
> 2 tablespoons soy sauce
> Salt and pepper to taste
> ½ cup finely chopped scallions, with tops
> 1 cup radish sprouts

1. Place the cabbage, daikon radish, and carrot into a large mixing bowl. Toss to blend well.

2. In a small mixing bowl, whisk the ginger, oil, vinegar, soy sauce, salt, and pepper together to form a smooth dressing. Add the scallions and stir again.

3. Pour the dressing over the vegetables and toss to blend well. Let rest for 15 minutes for the flavors to develop. Stir again. Garnish the salad with the radish sprouts and serve.

INDONESIAN VEGETABLE SALAD
WITH PEANUT SAUCE

>*3 large carrots, peeled*
>*3 medium taros or white potatoes, peeled*
>*3 medium turnips, peeled*
>*1 large green bell pepper, seeded*
>*2 medium zucchini squash*
>*4 large lettuce leaves for garnish*
>*1 teaspoon vegetable oil*
>*½ teaspoon ginger, minced*
>*3 scallions, finely chopped, tops included*
>*½ cup peanut butter, crunchy or smooth*
>*2 tablespoons soy sauce*
>*1 tablespoon lemon or lime juice*
>*½ teaspoon sugar*
>*Salt and pepper to taste*

1. Cut the carrots, taros, and turnips into large wedges about 2 inches long and ½ inch wide. Place in a pot of boiling water and cook for 10 minutes. Drain and cool.

2. Slice the peppers into long strips. Cut the zucchini into large wedges like the carrots and steam for 5 minutes. Drain and cool. Wash the lettuce and shred. Place lettuce on individual salad plates to form a bed.

3. In a medium saucepan, heat the oil over medium heat for 30

seconds. Add the ginger and scallions and cook, stirring often, for 1 minute.

4. Add the peanut butter, soy sauce, lemon juice, sugar, salt, and pepper and stir. Add enough water, about ¼ to ½ cup, and stir to form a creamy sauce.

5. Attractively arrange the carrots, taros, turnips, zucchini, and peppers on the plates of shredded lettuce. Spoon peanut sauce over all and serve.

COUSCOUS SALAD

> *1 cup couscous*
> *¾ cup boiling water*
> *1 small celery root or parsley root or 2 medium*
>   *parsnips*
> *1 medium carrot*
> *½ cup chopped scallions, tops included*
> *1 bunch red radishes, washed and sliced*
> *1 cup plain yogurt*
> *3 tablespoons lemon juice*
> *½ teaspoon cumin powder*
> *Salt and pepper to taste*

1. Place the couscous in a medium mixing bowl. Pour in boiling water and let stand for 15 minutes. Stir once to fluff and separate grains.

2. Peel and dice the celery root, parsley root, or parsnips, and the carrot. Cook in boiling water for 10 minutes until tender. Drain and cool.

3. Add the cooked vegetables, the scallions, and the sliced radishes to the couscous and toss to blend well.

4. Add the yogurt, lemon juice, cumin powder, salt, and pepper to the salad and stir to blend well. Serve with olives and pita bread.

ITALIAN WHITE BEAN
AND VEGETABLE SALAD

1 16-ounce can white beans
1 yellow or red sweet bell pepper, seeded and
  chopped
1 cup diced rutabaga
½ pound green beans
1 bunch red radishes
1 medium red onion, peeled and thinly sliced into
  rings
2 tablespoons red wine vinegar
Salt and pepper to taste
2 tablespoons minced fresh herbs such as basil,
  oregano, or parsley
½ cup olive oil

1. Drain and rinse the white beans. Place them in a medium mixing bowl. Add the bell pepper and stir gently.

2. Simmer the rutabaga and green beans in a saucepan of boiling water until tender-crisp, about 10 minutes. Drain, cool, and add to the white beans and bell pepper.

3. Thinly slice the radishes. Add radishes and onion to the vegetable mixture.

4. In a separate bowl, whisk together the vinegar, salt, pepper, minced fresh herbs, and olive oil to form a creamy dressing. Pour this over the bean and vegetable mixture and stir, being careful not to mash the beans. Serve.

OAXACAN BLACK BEAN AND VEGETABLE SALAD

> *1 16-ounce can black beans*
> *1 jicama, peeled and diced*
> *1 yellow or red sweet bell pepper, seeded and diced*
> *1 red Spanish onion, peeled and diced*
> *1 medium orange, peeled and thinly sliced*
> *1 small jalapeño or serrano pepper, seeded and minced*
> *2 tablespoons vegetable oil*
> *2 tablespoons orange juice*
> *½ cup minced fresh parsley*
> *½ teaspoon ground chili powder*
> *Salt and pepper to taste*

1. Rinse and drain the black beans. Place them in a large mixing bowl.

2. Add the jicama, bell pepper, onion, orange slices, and jalapeño pepper and toss to blend well.

3. Add the vegetable oil, orange juice, parsley, chili powder, salt, and pepper. Stir to blend well.

UNDERGROUND SALAD

> *2 medium parsnips*
> *1 small rutabaga*
> *1 small celery root*
> *½ cup chopped scallions*
> *2 cups cold chicken or turkey, diced*
> *½ cup sour cream*
> *½ cup mayonnaise*
> *Salt, pepper, and a dash of paprika to taste*

1. Peel the parsnips, rutabaga, and celery root with a stainless steel knife. Slice them into small, bite-sized pieces and cook in boiling water 10 minutes or until tender-crisp. Drain and rinse in cold water. Drain.

2. Place the roots in a medium mixing bowl. Add the scallions, chicken or turkey, sour cream, mayonnaise, salt, and pepper. Stir to blend well. Scoop into a serving bowl and sprinkle with a dash of paprika.

SEVICHE

Seviche is a Mexican dish of fish pickled in lemon or lime juice. It is a very refreshing salad that needs the crunch of some root vegetables.

> 1 pound bay scallops or thin-sliced sea scallops
> ¼ cup each fresh-squeezed lime juice and lemon juice
> 1 jicama, peeled and cut into very thin julienne strips
> 2 shallots, peeled and thinly sliced
> 1 jalapeño, serrano, or poblano pepper, seeded and minced
> 2 tablespoons minced cilantro or parsley
> Salt and pepper to taste

1. Place the scallops in a medium glass or pottery mixing bowl. Add the lemon and lime juice, jicama, shallots, and jalapeño. Stir to blend well. Cover and refrigerate for 1 hour.

2. Add the cilantro or parsley, salt, and pepper and stir to blend well. Serve.

WARM TURNIP GREENS SALAD FLORENTINE

> 2 large bunches fresh tender turnip greens
> 3 tablespoons extra-virgin olive oil
> 3 cloves garlic, peeled and minced
> Salt and freshly ground pepper to taste
> ½ cup grated Parmesan cheese

1. Carefully wash the turnip greens. Trim away any tough stems and chop the greens coarsely. Place them in a medium pot, add ½ cup water, cover, and steam/simmer for 10 minutes or until they are tender-crisp and still green. Drain and remove.

2. Return the pot to medium heat. Add the olive oil and garlic. Sauté for 3 minutes and add the turnip greens. Stir and toss to coat the greens with oil. Add salt and pepper to taste and serve on individual plates. Sprinkle with Parmesan cheese.

NOTE: If you find the turnip greens a little too tangy for your taste, substitute Italian-style escarole for half the turnip greens.

THAI BEEF AND VEGETABLE SALAD

3 medium carrots, peeled
5 to 6 large green lettuce leaves
¾ pound rare roast beef, thinly sliced
1½ cups shredded daikon radish
½ cup vegetable oil
1 tablespoon each fish sauce and soy sauce
⅓ cup minced fresh basil (Thai basil, if possible)
⅓ cup chopped roasted peanuts

1. Cut the carrots into wedges 2 inches long and ½ inch wide. Place in a saucepan and simmer over medium-high heat for 8 to 10 minutes until tender-crisp. Drain and reserve.

2. Wash and dry the lettuce leaves. Shred them and place them on individual salad plates. Layer the roast beef on the salad plates. Create a mound of daikon radish in the center of each salad plate.

3. Make the dressing by whisking together the oil, fish sauce, and soy sauce. Sprinkle the basil leaves and peanuts over the salad and drizzle with the dressing.

SWEET POTATO SALAD

4 large sweet potatoes
1 cup chopped celery stalks
1 cup chopped scallions
1 cup sour cream
⅓ cup mayonnaise
¼ cup minced fresh parsley
1 tablespoon fresh lemon juice
Salt and pepper to taste

1. Bake the sweet potatoes in a 350°F oven for 40 minutes. Remove, cool, and peel. Chop into bite-sized pieces. Place in a large mixing bowl.

2. Add the celery and scallions to the sweet potatoes and toss to blend well.

3. In a small mixing bowl, blend the sour cream, mayonnaise, parsley, lemon juice, salt and pepper to taste. Spoon into the bowl of sweet potatoes and toss to blend well.

Side Shows

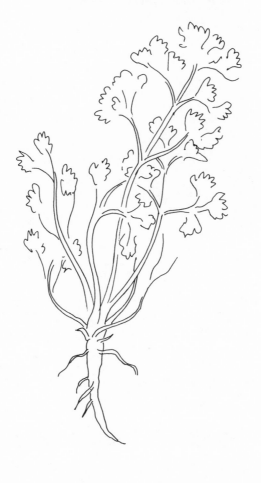

How many times have you tried to decide what side dish to serve along with the fried chicken, grilled hamburgers, or leftover ham that you already know you want to serve? You find yourself standing in the frozen food aisle staring at the hard little boxes of broccoli, chopped spinach, or peas and carrots.

Let the light bulb brighten in your mind and walk on over to the produce aisle and pick up some fresh beets, rutabaga, turnips, or parsnips and turn them into delicious, easy-to-prepare side dishes. Along with the main attraction, roots make great side show.

All of the recipes in this chapter will yield 4 to 6 servings.

POTATO AND PARSNIP PURÉE WITH PARSLEY

This dish, taught to me by my friend Phyllis, was a great hit at my all-*P* Christmas dinner. I served it with pork, peas, pumpkin pie, and Pinot Blanc.

> *4 medium white all-purpose potatoes*
> *4 parsnips*
> *3 tablespoons unsalted butter*
> *½ cup milk*
> *½ cup minced parsley*
> *Salt and pepper to taste*

1. Wash and peel the potatoes and parsnips. Cut them into chunks. Place them in a pot of boiling water and simmer for 20 minutes. Drain.

2. Add the butter, parsnips, potatoes, and milk to a food processor. (You can mash these roots with a potato masher if you prefer.) Process to a smooth purée.

3. Add the parsley, salt, and pepper and serve. Dot with extra butter if you like.

HOT BUTTERED BEETS

4 to 6 medium-sized beets, 2 to 2½ inches in
    diameter
2 tablespoons butter
Salt and pepper to taste

1. Wash the beets and trim off all but a ½-inch piece of the root and about a 1-inch piece of the leaf stems on top. Place the whole beets in a pot, cover with water, and turn the heat to high. Bring to a boil, reduce the heat to medium, and simmer for 25 to 30 minutes, maybe less if your beets are young and tender.

2. Drain the beets and let them cool enough so that you can handle them. Peel the beets and trim off the stems and roots. Slice the beets into wedges.

3. Melt the butter in a 2-quart saucepan over medium heat. Add the beets, salt, and pepper. Toss to coat with the butter and serve.

CARROT CUSTARD

1½ cups chopped carrots
1 cup half-and-half
½ cup heavy cream
3 large eggs
½ teaspoon finely minced fresh ginger
⅛ teaspoon salt
½ cup sugar

1. Preheat the oven to 325°F.

2. Place the chopped carrots in a saucepan, cover with water, and cook over high heat 8 to 10 minutes or until carrots are tender. Drain carrots, cool slightly, and purée in a food processor.

3. Pour the half-and-half and the heavy cream into a saucepan. Place the pan over medium heat until tiny bubbles form around the edge of the fluid. Don't boil. Remove and let cool.

4. In a medium mixing bowl, whip the eggs and ginger together.

Gradually add the scalded half-and-half and cream to the eggs, a tablespoon at a time at first. Stir to blend well. Add the carrot purée, the salt, and the sugar and blend well.

5. Pour the custard mixture into custard cups or ramekins and place them in a pan. Fill the pan with enough water to come halfway up the sides of the cups. Cover with a piece of foil and bake for 40 to 45 minutes or until a knife inserted into the center comes out clean.

6. Remove from oven and take the cups out of the water. Cool. Makes 6 carrot custards.

BUTTERED CARROT RINGS WITH LEMON

> *1½ pounds fresh carrots*
> *2 tablespoons unsalted butter or margarine*
> *Juice of 1 lemon*
> *1 tablespoon minced fresh parsley*
> *Salt and freshly ground pepper to taste*

1. Wash and peel the carrots. Slice the carrots into ¼-inch-thick rings.

2. Place the carrots in a saucepan and cover with water. Cover the pan and bring to a boil. Lower the heat to medium and simmer the carrots for 10 minutes or until they are tender but crisp.

3. Drain the carrots and return the pan to medium heat. Add the butter and lemon juice and cook for 3 minutes, stirring often. Add the parsley, salt, and pepper, stir and serve.

MINTED CARROT WEDGES

> *1½ pounds fresh carrots, washed and peeled*
> *2 tablespoons unsalted butter or margarine*
> *½ teaspoon sugar*
> *1 tablespoon minced fresh mint or 1 teaspoon dried*
> *Salt and pepper to taste*

1. Place a carrot horizontally in front of you on a cutting board. Hold a knife at a 45° angle and cut the carrot into diagonal wedges, rotating the carrot each time you make a cut.

2. Place the wedges in a saucepan, cover with water, and bring to a boil. Cover the pan, reduce the heat to medium, and simmer for 10 minutes or until crispy-tender.

3. Drain the carrots and return them to the saucepan over medium heat. Add the butter and sugar and cook, stirring often, for 3 minutes. Add the mint, salt, and pepper, stir, and serve.

GLAZED CARROTS WITH HONEY

1½ pounds fresh carrots, washed and peeled
2 tablespoons unsalted butter or margarine
2 tablespoons honey
Salt and pepper to taste

1. Cut the carrots into ½-inch dice. Start by slicing the whole carrots lengthwise into quarters. Reassemble the carrots and cut crosswise into diced chunks.

2. Place the carrots in a saucepan and cover with water. Bring to a boil, cover, reduce heat to medium, and simmer the carrots for 8 minutes or until crispy-tender. Drain.

3. Melt the butter and honey in the saucepan. Add the carrots, salt, and pepper. Stir and serve.

CARROTS JULIENNE À L'ORANGE

1½ pounds fresh carrots, washed and peeled
1 tablespoon butter or margarine
1 teaspoon cornstarch
½ cup orange juice
Salt and pepper to taste

1. Cut the carrots into 2- to 2½-inch-long sections. Cut these sections lengthwise in half, and then in half again. Slice each quarter carrot into matchsticks.

2. Place the carrots in a saucepan and cover with water. Bring to a boil, cover, reduce the heat to medium, and simmer for 8 minutes or until crispy-tender. Drain.

3. Melt the butter in the saucepan. Mix the cornstarch with the orange juice and stir carefully to remove any lumps.

4. Add the carrots to the butter. Add the salt and pepper. Add the orange juice mixture and simmer over medium-low heat for 3 minutes, stirring continuously, until a smooth sauce forms. Serve.

CARIBBEAN CARROT PURÉE

> 1½ pounds fresh carrots, washed and peeled
> 1 tablespoon vegetable oil
> 2 scallions, chopped
> 1 teaspoon minced fresh chili pepper, seeds removed
> 1 teaspoon minced fresh ginger or ¼ teaspoon powdered ginger
> ¼ teaspoon ground allspice
> Salt and pepper to taste

1. Chop the carrots coarsely and place them in a saucepan. Cover with water, bring to a boil, cover, reduce heat to medium, and simmer 10 minutes or until tender. Drain and cool slightly. Place in a food processor and purée.

2. Heat the oil in a saucepan over medium heat. Add the scallions and chili pepper. If the ginger is fresh, add that now, too, and sauté for 4 minutes. Add the spices, salt, and pepper and the carrots. Stir to blend well and serve.

CREAMED CARROTS WITH
SHALLOTS AND SNOW PEAS

¾ pound baby carrots, washed and trimmed
½ pound tiny snow peas or sugar snap peas
1 tablespoon butter or margarine
¼ cup minced fresh shallots or red onion
1 tablespoon all-purpose flour
1½ cups milk
Salt and pepper to taste

1. Place the carrots in a saucepan and cover with water. Bring to the boil, cover, reduce heat to medium, and simmer 5 minutes until carrots are tender-crisp.

2. Add the peas to the carrots, cover, and simmer for 3 minutes. Drain.

3. Melt the butter in a saucepan over medium heat. Add the shallots and sauté for 3 minutes. Add the flour and stir carefully for 1 minute. Add the milk and stir to form a creamy sauce.

4. Add the carrots and peas to the sauce. Add the salt and pepper to taste. Stir and serve.

CELERIAC AU GRATIN

2 medium celeriacs
2 tablespoons butter
2 tablespoons all-purpose flour
1 cup milk
Salt and pepper to taste
½ cup grated cheese—Cheddar, Swiss, Parmesan,
   your choice
½ cup dry bread crumbs or crushed crackers
½ teaspoon paprika

1. Boil the celeriac in water to cover for 20 to 25 minutes or until quite soft. Drain, cool, and peel. Mash.

2. In a saucepan, melt the butter over medium heat. Add the flour

and stir to form a roux. Add the milk and salt and pepper, and stir over medium-high heat to form a creamy sauce.

3. Add the celeriac to the sauce and stir to blend well. Place in a casserole dish. Mix the cheese, bread crumbs, and paprika. Sprinkle over the mashed celeriac and place in a 375°F oven for 10 minutes to form a golden crust.

CREAMED CELERIAC WITH CARAWAY

2 medium celeriacs
2 tablespoons butter
½ cup minced red onion
2 tablespoons all-purpose flour
1 cup milk
1 teaspoon caraway seeds
Salt and pepper to taste

1. Boil the celeriacs in a large pot of water for 20 to 25 minutes or until quite soft. Drain, cool, and peel. Chop the celeriacs into ½-inch-square chunks.

2. Melt the butter in a medium saucepan over medium heat. Add the minced onion and sauté for 3 to 5 minutes. Add the flour and stir to form a roux. Add the milk and stir to form a creamy sauce.

3. Add the caraway seeds, salt, pepper, and celeriac. Cook over low heat for 10 minutes. You may have to add a little bit more milk if the sauce gets too thick.

CELERIAC ITALIANO

2 medium celeriacs
3 tablespoons olive oil
2 cloves garlic
2 tablespoons fresh minced parsley
1 tablespoon red wine vinegar
Salt and freshly ground black pepper to taste

1. Peel celeriacs and grate in the food processor. Heat the olive oil in a large heavy skillet over medium heat for 1 minute. Add the celeriac and sauté for 5 minutes.

2. Add the garlic and sauté for 1 minute. Add the parsley, vinegar, salt, and pepper and sauté for 1 more minute.

3. Spoon the celeriacs onto a platter and let cool to room temperature before serving.

CELERIAC AND POTATO PURÉE

1 medium celeriac
3 medium white potatoes
2 tablespoons butter
½ cup milk or half-and-half
2 tablespoons fresh minced parsley or chervil (optional)
Salt and pepper to taste

1. Peel and chop the celeriac into chunks. Peel and chop the potatoes into chunks. Put the celeriac and potatoes in a saucepan and cover with water. Boil the vegetables 10 to 15 minutes or until soft.

2. Drain and mash the vegetables. Add the butter, milk, parsley, salt, and pepper. Whip to form a purée.

FRIED PARSNIP CAKES

2 pounds parsnips, peeled and coarsely chopped
2 eggs, well beaten
⅓ cup flour
1 tablespoon minced fresh parsley
½ teaspoon each salt and freshly ground black pepper
⅛ teaspoon ground mace
4 to 6 tablespoons unsalted butter

1. Place the parsnips in a pot of water and boil till tender, about 15 minutes. Drain and mash, or drain and put through a food processor.

2. Scrape the parsnips into a mixing bowl. Stir in the eggs, flour, parsley, the salt and pepper, and mace. Blend well and refrigerate, covered, about 30 minutes.

3. Coat your hands with flour and form the parsnip batter into small cakes, 2½ inches round by ½ inch thick. Sauté the cakes in the melted butter about 6 minutes on each side till golden brown. Makes about a dozen cakes. Wonderful with roast chicken.

SKILLET-GRILLED PARSNIPS

> *2 pounds parsnips*
> *2 tablespoons butter, margarine, or olive oil*
> *¼ cup water*
> *Salt and pepper to taste*

1. Wash and peel the parsnips. Use a very sharp knife and slice the parsnips lengthwise into long, slender strips about ¼ inch thick.

2. Heat a large, heavy skillet over medium heat for 3 minutes. Add half the parsnips, half the butter, and half the water. Cover and steam-sauté for 5 minutes. Remove cover, turn the parsnips, and continue cooking until brown. Repeat with the other half. Sprinkle with salt and pepper to taste.

SKILLET-BRAISED RUTABAGA

> *1 large rutabaga*
> *2 tablespoons butter*
> *¼ cup water*
> *Salt and pepper to taste*

1. Wash the rutabaga and peel off the waxy coating. Cut the

rutabaga in half and then in half again. Cut the quarters into ½-inch slices and cut the slices into wedges.

2. Melt the butter in a heavy cast iron skillet and add the rutabaga and water. Cover and simmer over medium heat for 15 minutes. Remove the lid and add the salt and pepper. Continue cooking for another 10 to 15 minutes, stirring occasionally, until the roots are tender and browned all over.

BOILED RUTABAGA WITH BUTTER AND PARSLEY

> *1 large rutabaga*
> *1 tablespoon butter*
> *1 tablespoon fresh minced parsley*
> *Salt and pepper to taste*

1. Peel the rutabaga. If you are dexterous with a peeler, use that. If not, cut the rutabaga in half at the equator, or in hemispheres. A whole raw rutabaga can be difficult to cut in half because it is so firm. Lay the large side facedown and peel with a sharp knife. Continue to cut the root into ½- to 1-inch chunks.

2. Place the chunks in a pan and cover with water. Bring to the boil, cover, and reduce heat to medium. Simmer for 15 to 20 minutes or until tender-crisp.

3. Drain the water from the pan. Add the butter, parsley, salt, and pepper and return to medium heat. Stir constantly for 1 minute or until butter melts and coats the roots.

CANDIED RUTABAGA

> *1 large or two small rutabagas*
> *3 tablespoons water*
> *Salt and freshly ground black pepper to taste*

¾ cup light or dark brown sugar
2 tablespoons butter

1. Preheat oven to 375°F.

2. Peel the rutabaga and cut into quarters. Cut the quarters into wedges that resemble sweet potato wedges.

3. Place the wedges in a shallow baking dish along with the water. Sprinkle with salt, pepper, and brown sugar. Dot with butter.

3. Bake in the oven, covered, for 15 minutes. Uncover, stir, and bake an additional 10 to 15 minutes or until glazed.

CREAMY RUTABAGA WITH CARAWAY

1 large rutabaga
1 tablespoon butter
1 tablespoon all-purpose flour
1½ cups milk
½ teaspoon caraway seeds
Salt and pepper to taste

1. Peel the rutabaga and cut into bite-sized pieces. Place in a pot and cover with water. Bring to a boil, cover, reduce heat to medium low, and simmer for 15 minutes or until roots are tender-crisp. Drain.

2. Meanwhile, make the cream sauce in a separate pan. Over medium heat, melt the butter. Add the flour and stir to blend well. Stir the roux constantly over medium heat for 2 to 3 minutes. Add the milk and whisk to break up any lumps. Cook the sauce for 5 minutes, stirring frequently to form a creamy sauce.

3. Add the caraway, salt, and pepper to the cream sauce. Stir. Add the rutabaga and stir.

CHEESY CREAMY BAKED RUTABAGA

1 large rutabaga
1 tablespoon all-purpose flour
Salt and pepper to taste
Pinch of nutmeg or mace
¾ cup grated plain, dilled, or caraway Havarti
  cheese
2 cups milk
1½ cups rye bread crumbs

1. Preheat the oven to 375°F.

2. Peel the waxy coating off the rutabaga and cut it in half. Cut the halves into very thin slices. Arrange the slices in a casserole and sprinkle with flour, salt, pepper, and nutmeg.

3. Arrange the cheese on top of the rutabaga, pour the milk over and sprinkle with bread crumbs. (Make rye bread crumbs by lightly toasting and crumbling fresh rye bread or simply crumbling day-old rye bread.)

4. Cover the casserole and bake in the oven for ½ hour. Uncover and bake for an additional 10 to 15 minutes.

SKILLET-BRAISED TURNIPS FRANÇAISE

1 tablespoon olive oil
1 pound young turnips, peeled and cubed
¼ cup chicken stock or water
¼ teaspoon salt
Freshly ground black pepper to taste
2 tablespoons unsalted butter
1 tablespoon minced fresh parsley

1. In a heavy skillet, heat the olive oil and add the turnips. Sauté over medium-high heat for 3 to 4 minutes. Add the stock or water, cover, and turn the heat down very low. Cook for 10 minutes.

2. Uncover the skillet, return the heat to high, add the salt and

pepper, and sauté the turnips for 2 minutes. Add the butter and sauté till the butter melts. Serve with the minced parsley.

TURNIP CUPS WITH PEAS AND HAM

4 medium-sized turnips
2 tablespoons butter
2 tablespoons all-purpose flour
2 to 2½ cups milk
1 cup fresh or frozen peas
1 cup chopped cured ham
Salt and pepper to taste
Dash of paprika

1. Find 4 turnips of the same size and without any blemishes. Carefully peel and slice in half. Put the halves in a pot of water to cover and simmer over medium heat until tender-crisp, about 10 minutes. Test with a sharp knife. You want them to be tender but still sturdy enough to hold the filling.

2. Drain the turnips and wait until cool enough to handle. Carefully scoop out the center of the turnips to form cups. Finely chop the scoopings and set aside.

3. Melt the butter over medium heat in a 2-quart saucepan. Add the flour and stir to form a roux or paste. Stir continuously and cook over medium heat for 2 minutes. Add the milk and whisk to break up any lumps. Stir to form a creamy sauce.

4. Add the turnip scoopings, peas, and ham to the sauce. Add the salt and pepper. Stir and cook over medium heat for 5 minutes.

5. Place the turnip cups in a casserole dish and fill with the sauce. Place in a 375°F oven for 10 minutes and serve.

MEDITERRANEAN TURNIPS WITH TOMATOES

1 tablespoon olive oil
1 small onion, chopped fine
2 cloves garlic, minced
4 medium turnips, peeled and chopped into bite-sized wedges
1 large tomato, peeled and chopped
1 tablespoon minced fresh or 1 teaspoon dry basil
1 teaspoon capers (optional)
1 tablespoon chopped pitted green or black olives (optional)
Salt and pepper to taste

1. Place the olive oil in a medium saucepan and heat over medium-high heat for 1 minute. Add the onion, garlic, and turnips. Sauté for 3 minutes, stirring occasionally.

2. Add the tomatoes, basil, capers, olives, salt, and pepper. Cover and simmer for 15 minutes.

SOUTHERN TURNIP GREENS WITH TURNIPS

2 pounds turnip greens
2 medium turnips
3 ounces slab bacon or bacon strips
Freshly ground black pepper

1. Carefully wash the turnip greens to remove any sand or grit that can get stuck in the leaves. Strip the soft, fleshy leaves from the stems and discard the stems. Chop the leaves into ½-inch-wide strips.

2. Wash and peel the turnips. Chop into very small slivers. Cut the bacon into ¼- to ½-inch-wide pieces and place in a large stainless steel or other noncorrosive pot. Sauté the bacon until slightly crisp and drippings have appeared.

3. Add the greens to the bacon, cover with water, and bring to a boil. Turn the heat to medium and simmer for 20 minutes. Add the turnip slivers and simmer for another 10 minutes.

4. Season with pepper and serve.

GRILLED VEGETABLES

> *2 large sweet potatoes, malanga, or Idaho potatoes*
> *3 large sweet onions such as Vidalia, Imperial, or Walla Walla*
> *2 turnips*
> *2 celery roots or parsley roots or parsnips*
> *1 rutabaga*
> *1 cup olive or vegetable oil*
> *Juice of 1 lemon*
> *1 tablespoon fresh minced thyme or rosemary or combination*
> *Salt and pepper to taste*

1. Build a bed of coals in a kettle-type charcoal grill with a lid or heat a gas-fired grill. Place a fine metal grilling screen over the regular rack and brush with vegetable oil.

2. Wash and peel all the vegetables. Slice the Idaho potatoes, sweet potatoes, or malanga in half lengthwise. Slice the onions and turnips in half crosswise. Slice the celery root and rutabaga into ½-inch-thick chunks. Slice the parsley roots or parsnips in half lengthwise.

3. Place the vegetables in a large mixing bowl or roasting pan. Drizzle the oil and lemon juice over all. Sprinkle with the minced herbs, salt, and pepper. Stir to coat the vegetables with the oil.

4. Place the vegetables on the grill and cook until soft and tender. Turn often and baste with remaining oil marinade.

5. Remove from the grill, cut into chunks, and serve.

SWEET POTATO SOUFFLÉ

> 3 large sweet potatoes
> ¼ cup each white and light brown sugar
> ½ cup hot milk
> 2 eggs, separated

1. Bake, boil, or microwave the sweet potatoes. Peel and mash. Place in a medium mixing bowl.

2. Add the sugars and hot milk and stir. Add the egg yolks and whip until fluffy. Beat the egg whites until stiff and add to the mixture, folding carefully.

3. Pour into a buttered baking dish and bake in a 350°F oven for 20 to 30 minutes or until lightly browned on top. Serve immediately with pork roast.

SCALLOPED POTATOES, SALSIFY, AND RUTABAGA

> 3 medium white or red all-purpose potatoes
> 1 or 2 salsify roots
> 1 medium rutabaga
> 3 tablespoons all-purpose flour
> 3 cups whole milk
> 2 tablespoons butter
> Salt and pepper to taste

1. Peel and thinly slice the potatoes, salsify, and rutabaga. Layer half of them in a buttered baking dish. Sprinkle with flour and stir to coat. Repeat with the other half.

2. Warm the milk but do not boil and pour over the potatoes, salsify, and rutabaga. Dot with butter and sprinkle with salt and pepper.

3. Cover with foil and bake in a 375°F oven for 30 minutes. Remove the foil, reduce the heat to 350°F and bake another 10 to 15 minutes until crust is golden brown.

CARIBBEAN BONIATO AND FRUIT COMPOTE

1 large or 2 medium boniato (Cuban sweet potatoes)
1 medium banana
1 small pineapple or 1 16-ounce can pineapple chunks
¼ cup raisins
2 tablespoons honey
⅓ cup orange juice or reserved pineapple juice

1. Peel and slice the boniato, banana, and pineapple into thick slices. Toss to mix and place in a small baking dish.

2. Sprinkle with raisins, honey, and juice. Cover with foil and bake in a 350°F oven for 1 hour. Serve with rice and jerked pork.

PORTUGUESE POTATOES O'BRIEN

¼ to ½ pound linguiça or chorizo sausage
2 tablespoons olive oil, extra if necessary
4 to 5 medium white all-purpose potatoes
¼ cup each sweet red and green bell pepper, minced
¼ cup minced onion
Salt and pepper to taste

1. Chop the linguiça or chorizo sausage and sauté it in a large frying pan over medium heat for 15 minutes.

2. Peel and dice the potatoes and simmer them in hot water for 10 minutes. Drain.

3. Add the potatoes to the frying pan with the sausage. Add more oil if necessary. Add the red and green bell peppers and the onion. Sauté for 10 minutes, stirring occasionally.

4. Add the salt and pepper to taste, stir, and serve.

RAGOUT OF ONIONS

This is a rich-tasting side dish for when the cupboard is bare or if you just plain love onions.

4 large onions, red and/or white
2 tablespoons butter or vegetable oil
2 tablespoons all-purpose flour
2 cups beef stock or broth, heated
2 tablespoons minced fresh chives, parsley, summer
savory, or combination
Salt and pepper to taste

1. Peel and thinly slice the onions. Melt the butter in a large, heavy skillet over medium heat and fry the onions until soft, about 10 minutes.

2. Sprinkle the flour over the onions and stir. Cook, stirring often, for 2 minutes.

3. Add the broth and stir to form a creamy ragout. Sprinkle with fresh herbs, salt and pepper to taste, and serve.

SEVEN

Stews

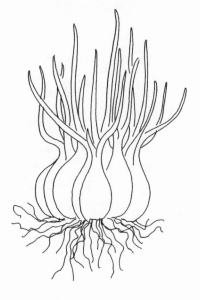

Frosty weather, a wood-burning cookstove, and a big caldron of simmering stew make a picture of what Currier and Ives thought American life should be. Root vegetables are just as much a part of this American idyll as the horse-drawn sleigh and the apple pie for dessert. It just so happens that root vegetables are at their peak of perfection and delectability just when the snow starts to fall.

This chapter will highlight the importance of roots in Irish and American stews and goulash, as well as in pot pies, cobblers, and other casseroles.

All of the recipes in this chapter will yield 4 to 6 servings.

WINTER ROOTS BEEF STEW

> *2 pounds beef for stew, cut into bite-sized chunks*
> *¼ cup all-purpose flour*
> *½ teaspoon each salt and pepper*
> *3 tablespoons butter or vegetable oil*
> *2½ cups beef broth or water*
> *1 tablespoon Worcestershire sauce*
> *10 tiny white onions, peeled*
> *2 carrots, peeled and cut into chunks*
> *8 small new white or red potatoes*

1. Place beef, flour, salt, and pepper in a mixing bowl. Toss to coat the beef with the seasoned flour.

2. Heat butter or oil in a heavy stewpot over medium heat for 2 minutes. Add beef chunks a few at a time and fry until browned all over. Remove and repeat until all beef chunks are done.

3. Add beef broth or water and Worcestershire sauce and stir.

Return beef to the pot, cover, reduce heat to low, and simmer for 1½ hours or until meat is tender.

4. Add the onions, carrots, and potatoes and cook another 25 to 30 minutes. Serve.

NOTE: Feel free to substitute turnips, rutabaga, celery root, or parsley root to make your own favorite beef stew.

AUNT BEE'S GERMAN ROOTS GOULASH

> *2 tablespoons butter or vegetable oil*
> *1 medium onion*
> *2 tablespoons all-purpose flour*
> *2 cups warm milk*
> *2 cups fresh or frozen corn kernels*
> *1 cup each diced potato, turnip, and rutabaga*
> *½ pound ground pork*
> *1 egg*
> *¼ teaspoon mace*
> *1 tablespoon fresh minced summer savory*
> * (optional)*
> *2 tablespoons bread crumbs*
> *Salt and pepper to taste*

1. Melt the butter or oil in a medium soup pot over medium heat for 1 minute. Add the onion and fry for 3 minutes, stirring often.

2. Sprinkle the flour over the onion and cook, stirring often, for 3 minutes. Add the warm milk and stir to form a creamy sauce. Add the corn.

3. Place the diced roots in a pot of boiling water for 5 minutes. Drain and add to the pot of cream sauce. Simmer over medium heat.

4. Place the pork, egg, mace, summer savory, and bread crumbs in a small mixing bowl. Form into tiny meatballs, about the size of a small white grape. Drop the meatballs into the simmering goulash and cook for 10 minutes. Season with salt and pepper. Add a little milk to the goulash if it starts to get too thick.

5. Serve in bowls with rye bread, butter, and pickles.

VEAL AND PARSNIP COBBLER

1½ pounds veal for stew
6 tablespoons all-purpose flour
½ teaspoon each salt and pepper
¼ teaspoon paprika
3 tablespoons butter or vegetable oil
3 cups hot beef or chicken broth or water
1 stalk celery, chopped
4 parsnips, peeled and diced
1 package refrigerated biscuit dough or your favorite
  biscuit recipe or
2 cups sifted flour
½ teaspoon salt
1 tablespoon baking powder
¼ cup shortening
1 cup milk

1. Place the veal, flour, salt, pepper, and paprika in a bowl. Dredge the veal in the flour until well coated.

2. Heat the butter or oil in a large, heavy stew pot and fry the veal chunks a few at a time until browned all over. Remove and repeat with all the veal.

3. Pour the broth or water into the pot and stir. Return the veal to the pot, reduce heat to medium low, cover, and simmer for 1½ hours.

4. Add the celery and parsnips and simmer for 15 minutes. Place the veal stew in a large casserole.

5. To make biscuits, mix the dry ingredients together. Cut in the shortening with a fork until the dough resembles coarse crumbs. Add the milk and stir quickly to form a sticky dough. Drop the dough by the teaspoonful on to the veal. Place in a 350°F oven for 15 minutes or until the biscuits are browned. Serve.

CELERIAC AND SHRIMP CREOLE

1 medium celeriac
½ pound shrimp
2 tablespoons olive or other vegetable oil
1 medium onion, peeled and chopped fine
1 medium green or red bell pepper, cored and chopped
½ cup fresh minced parsley
½ cup chopped green scallions
½ teaspoon cayenne pepper
½ teaspoon dried thyme
3 medium tomatoes, chopped, or 1 28-ounce can tomatoes, crushed
Salt and pepper to taste

1. Peel and chop the celeriac. Peel and devein the shrimp. In a large pot, heat the oil over medium-high heat for 1 minute. Add the celeriac, onion, and bell pepper and sauté for 8 minutes or until tender.

2. Add the parsley, scallions, cayenne, and thyme. Stir and sauté for 1 minute. Add the tomatoes, salt, and pepper. Cook for 5 minutes. Add the shrimp and cook another 5 minutes. Let rest 5 minutes and serve over white rice.

CORNED BEEF AND PARSNIP HASH

2 tablespoons olive or other vegetable oil
1 medium onion, minced
3 large parsnips, peeled and grated
2 cups shredded corned beef or roast beef
½ cup milk or cream
Salt and pepper to taste

1. Warm the olive oil in a large, heavy skillet over medium heat for 2 minutes. Add the onion and sauté for 2 minutes.

2. Add the parsnips, corned beef, milk or cream, salt, and pepper. Fry over medium heat 5 to 10 minutes or until browned on one side. Turn the hash over and fry till crispy and browned on the other side.

RUTABAGA CHOUCROUTE

> *1 medium-sized rutabaga*
> *2 ounces salt pork or slab bacon, cut into chunks*
> *1 small onion, minced*
> *1 8-ounce package sauerkraut, rinsed and drained*
> *2 cups dry white wine, preferably Riesling*
> *1 bay leaf*
> *½ teaspoon ground mace*
> *Salt and pepper to taste*
> *2 smoked pork chops*
> *2 each cooked bratwurst or weisswurst, knock-*
> * wurst, and frankfurters*

1. Peel the rutabaga and chop into ½- to 1-inch chunks.

2. In a 9-inch skillet or pot with a tight-fitting lid, sauté the salt pork or bacon over medium heat for 2 minutes. Add the onion and rutabaga and sauté another minute.

3. Add the sauerkraut, wine, bay leaf, mace, salt, and pepper. Bring the kraut to a boil, reduce the heat to medium-low, cover, and simmer 30 minutes. Lift the lid occasionally and add more wine or water if it gets too dry.

4. Add the smoked chops and sausages, cover, and simmer for 15 minutes. Spoon the kraut and rutabaga onto a platter in separate piles as much as possible. Layer the meats on top and serve with two or three different mustards, bread, and more wine.

RUTABAGA SHEPHERD'S PIE

1 small rutabaga
2 medium white potatoes
½ cup milk or half-and-half
2 tablespoons butter
2 shoulder lamb chops
1 tablespoon olive oil or vegetable oil
1 small onion, peeled and chopped
1 cup green beans, fresh or frozen
½ cup chopped celery
1 cup chopped zucchini, fresh or frozen
1 tablespoon all-purpose flour
1½ cups beef stock or beef stock and water
1 tablespoon Worcestershire sauce
Salt and pepper to taste

1. Make the mashed rutabaga and potatoes. Peel and dice the rutabaga and potatoes and boil together until soft. Drain. Add the milk and butter and mash to a smooth purée.

2. Trim the fat and bone away from the shoulder lamb chops and slice into bite-sized pieces. Sauté the lamb in a large skillet until browned all over.

3. Add the onions, green beans, celery, and zucchini and sauté for 3 to 4 minutes. Sprinkle the flour over the meat and stir. Pour the stock over all and stir to form a creamy gravy. Season with Worcestershire sauce, salt, and pepper.

4. Pour the meat and vegetables into a casserole and cover with the mashed rutabaga. Bake at 350°F for 30 minutes.

CURRIED CHICKEN WITH RUTABAGA AND PEAS

2 tablespoons vegetable oil
1 large white, yellow, or red onion, chopped
3 cloves garlic, peeled and minced

6 chicken thighs or legs
3 tablespoons curry powder
1 rutabaga, peeled and diced
1 28-ounce can whole or chopped tomatoes
Salt and pepper to taste
1 10-ounce package frozen peas

1. Warm the vegetable oil in a 4-quart pot over medium heat for 1 minute. Add the chopped onion and fry for 2 minutes. Add the garlic and fry for 2 minutes more. Add the chicken parts and fry for 10 minutes, turning the chicken often to brown all over.

2. Add the curry powder and fry for 1 minute. Add the rutabaga, tomatoes, salt, and pepper. Add water if necessary to just cover all ingredients. Cover the pot, bring to a boil, reduce heat to medium, and simmer for 30 minutes. Stir occasionally.

3. Add the frozen peas and cook for 10 minutes. Serve with plain white rice and mango chutney.

CURRIED PORK WITH TURNIPS

1 pound boneless pork, cut into ½- to ¾-inch cubes
2 tablespoons all-purpose flour
2 tablespoons vegetable oil
1 large onion, chopped
2 medium turnips, peeled and diced
2 cloves garlic, minced
1 tablespoon curry powder
1½ cups canned tomato sauce
2 tablespoons currants or raisins
Salt and pepper to taste

1. Dredge the pork in the flour in a medium-sized bowl. Shake to remove any excess flour. Heat the vegetable oil in a wide, heavy skillet for 1 minute. Add the pork chunks and fry till browned all over, about 5 minutes.

2. Remove pork from skillet. Add the onion, turnips, and garlic to

the skillet and fry for 2 minutes. Add the curry powder and fry another minute. Stir in the pork, tomato sauce, currants, salt, and pepper. Cover the pan and simmer for 30 minutes, adding more water if the stew gets too dry.

BANGERS AND BASHED NEEPS, A.K.A.
ENGLISH SAUSAGES AND MASHED TURNIPS

1 teaspoon vegetable oil
1 pound English sausages, available at some specialty stores, or substitute mild white breakfast sausages, weisswurst, or cooked bratwurst
3 medium turnips, peeled and chopped
1 medium white potato, peeled and chopped
2 tablespoons butter
½ cup cream, half-and-half, or milk
Salt and pepper to taste

1. Fry the sausages in a teaspoon of oil over medium-low heat for 10 minutes, or broil in the oven 6 inches from the heat source for 5 minutes, turning often, or drop the sausages in a pot of boiling water, reduce heat to medium-low, and simmer for 5 minutes.

2. Place the turnips and potato in a pot of water and boil 15 to 20 minutes or until quite soft. Drain and add butter, cream, salt, and pepper.

3. Mash with a potato masher or place in a food processor and pulse quickly. I like to leave my neeps a little lumpy and prefer them bashed with a hand masher.

4. Serve the sausages and neeps on a plate with Colman's English mustard, wheat bread, sweet butter, a pint of bitter, and a wedge of Stilton for dessert.

ITALIAN SAUSAGE WITH PARSNIPS AND TOMATOES

> *4 to 6 sweet Italian sausages, about 1 pound*
> *1 pound parsnips, peeled and cut into ¼-inch-thick*
> *rings*
> *1 medium onion, chopped*
> *3 cloves garlic, minced*
> *1 medium green or red pepper, chopped*
> *2 tablespoons flat leaf parsley, minced*
> *1 tablespoon fresh or 1 teaspoon dried oregano*
> *1 tablespoon fresh or 1 teaspoon dried basil*
> *1 28-ounce can whole or crushed tomatoes*
> *Salt and pepper to taste*

1. Sauté the sausages in a large skillet over medium heat for 15 minutes. Turn often to make them browned all over. Add the parsnips and stir to coat with the rendered sausage fat.

2. Add the onions, garlic, peppers, parsley, oregano, basil, tomatoes, salt, and pepper. Cover the skillet and simmer for 30 minutes.

MAPLED HAM AND SWEET POTATO CASSEROLE

> *1 center-cut slice of ham or about 1½ pounds other*
> *baked ham*
> *3 medium sweet potatoes, peeled and sliced ¼ inch*
> *thick*
> *4 tart apples, cored and cut into chunks or slices*
> *¾ cup warm water or a blend of water and dry white*
> *wine*
> *½ cup pure maple syrup*
> *¼ teaspoon each salt and pepper*
> *2 tablespoons butter*

1. Arrange the ham, sweet potatoes, and apples in alternating

rows in a casserole dish. Pour the water or water and wine mixture over the food. Drizzle the maple syrup over that. Season with salt and pepper. Dot with butter, cover with foil, and bake in a 350°F oven for 30 minutes.

2. Remove the foil cover and let brown in the oven for 15 minutes.

MEXICAN VEGETABLE STEW, A.K.A. PUCHERO ESPAÑOL

> *4 chicken wings*
> *2 strips slab bacon, chopped*
> *2 chorizo sausages*
> *½ pound beef for stew, cut in 1-inch-thick chunks*
> *⅛ teaspoon ground cloves*
> *4 to 6 strands saffron*
> *1 cup canned garbanzo beans, drained*
> *2 cloves garlic, minced*
> *2 carrots, peeled and chopped in circles*
> *2 turnips, peeled and cut in ½-inch chunks*
> *1 medium onion, peeled and chopped*
> *1 teaspoon mild red chili powder*
> *2 cups shredded cabbage*
> *Salt and pepper to taste*

1. Place the chicken wings, bacon, sausage, and beef in a large pot. Cover with water, bring to a boil, reduce heat to medium, cover, and simmer for 30 minutes.

2. Add the rest of the ingredients and simmer for another 30 minutes.

3. Separate the meat from the vegetables. Chop the meat into serving pieces and give each person a portion of each. Drain the vegetables and garbanzo beans and give a portion to each on the same plate.

4. Serve the soup from the pot in bowls.

CHICKEN AND ROOTS POT PIE

1 3½- to 4-pound chicken
½ cup diced onion
½ cup diced carrot
½ cup diced turnip
½ cup diced parsnip
4 tablespoons butter or vegetable oil
4 tablespoons all-purpose flour
2 cups chicken broth
Salt and pepper to taste
1 frozen or prepared pastry or pie crust

1. Place the chicken in a 4-quart soup pot and cover with water. Bring the water to the boil, reduce heat to medium, and simmer for 30 to 40 minutes. Remove scum as it rises to the surface.

2. Remove chicken from the pot. Remove the skin and bones and discard. Chop the remaining chicken into chunks.

3. Reheat the chicken stock and add the vegetables. Simmer over medium-high heat for 5 minutes. Remove the vegetables and keep warm.

4. In a 2-quart saucepan, melt the butter over medium heat. Add the flour and stir to form a paste. Add the chicken broth and stir to form a creamy and thick sauce. Season with salt and pepper.

5. Fill a casserole with the chicken and add the vegetables. Pour the sauce over all. Top with a pastry crust. Make slits in the crust to allow steam to escape. Bake the pie in a 350°F oven for 25 minutes or until the crust is golden brown.

ONION VEGETABLE TART

CRUST
1 cup all-purpose flour
¼ teaspoon salt
¼ pound unsalted butter
¼ to ⅓ cup ice water
FILLING
1 tablespoon butter or olive oil
2 medium sweet onions such as Walla Walla, Vidalia, etc., thinly sliced
1 cup each finely chopped parsnip and carrot
1½ cups milk, warmed
3 eggs
1 cup shredded Swiss or Gruyère cheese or any cheese you like

1. Make the crust by mixing together the flour, salt, and unsalted butter until it resembles coarse bread crumbs. Add water and stir to form a ball of dough. Roll the dough to fit a 9-inch pie pan.

2. Melt the butter in a heavy skillet over medium heat. Add the onions, parsnip, and carrot. Fry over medium heat for 8 to 10 minutes or until soft. Let cool and place the vegetables in the pie shell.

3. In a separate bowl, blend the warm milk, the eggs, and the cheese. Pour over the vegetables.

4. Bake the pie in a 450°F oven for 10 minutes. Reduce heat to 325°F and bake another 20 minutes or until filling is firm and golden brown on top.

EIGHT

Roasted Roots
and Other Entrees

One early-October afternoon many years ago, when I was in college in Illinois, several of my friends and I decided to pack up the old car and head for the wilds of southwest Wisconsin. We had a great time getting there, but being college kids, we forgot to bring along any food.

Luckily, we were able to gather a few beets pulled from a friend's garden near Boscobel, Wisconsin. As we gathered around the campfire to watch the moon rise, we all realized we were hungry. What's to eat? Beets. That's all? That's right.

We tossed the beets in the campfire, stirred them with a stick once in a while, and then pulled them out when we thought they were done. They were magnificent. The smoky campfire had imparted an incredible flavor once we were able to peel off the charred crust that had formed on the outside.

This chapter starts with that taste memory and charts a course through other baked and roasted roots dishes plus some that are simmered on the stove. Many you will recognize as favorites, some with added twists.

All of the recipes in this chapter will yield 4 to 6 servings.

MARIE'S BOILED ROOTS DINNER

> *1 pound chuck roast or beef for stew*
> *2 turnips, peeled and cut in eighths*
> *1 small rutabaga, peeled and diced*
> *2 carrots, peeled and cut in circles ½ inch thick*
> *2 cups chopped cabbage*
> *2 cups drained sauerkraut*
> *Salt and pepper to taste*

1. Place the beef in the bottom of a large pot with a tight-fitting lid. Place the turnips, rutabaga, carrots, and cabbage on top and around the meat. Place the sauerkraut on top of that and cover with water.

2. Bring the contents to the boil and reduce heat to low and simmer for 60 minutes. Remove the meat from the pot and cut into serving chunks.

3. Place the meat and vegetables on a platter in separate piles if possible. The idea is to place a little bit of everything on everybody's plate and then mash the roots with the back of your fork. Pass the salt and pepper at the table. Serve with rye or pumpernickel bread and sweet butter.

ROASTED ROOTS WITH FRESH ROSEMARY

4 medium beets
2 large Idaho potatoes or 3 to 4 medium white,
*   yellow, or red potatoes*
2 parsnips
3 carrots
2 medium to large turnips
5 cloves garlic or shallots, unpeeled
¼ cup chopped fresh rosemary or fresh thyme
¼ cup olive oil
Salt and pepper to taste

1. Peel the beets, potatoes, parsnips, carrots, and turnips. Cut the potatoes in half if they are very large and leave the other roots whole. Place them in a roasting pan or casserole dish just large enough to hold them.

2. Strategically place the garlic cloves or shallots around the roots so they are evenly dispersed. You can add more garlic or shallots if you want to.

3. Sprinkle the rosemary or thyme, olive oil, salt, and pepper over

the roots. Cover with foil and bake at 375°F for 30 minutes. Remove cover and bake for another 15 minutes or until roots are browned and tender.

BAKED CHICKEN OR TURKEY WITH ROOTS STUFFING

1 10- to 12- pound turkey
½ pound lightly seasoned ground pork sausage
3 tablespoons butter or olive oil
1 medium onion
1 each carrot, small celery root, parsnip, and turnip,
  peeled and grated
2 cloves garlic, peeled and minced
1 tart apple, cored and chopped fine
½ cup fresh minced parsley
4 cups soft whole wheat bread crumbs
½ teaspoon each salt and pepper
1 tablespoon thyme leaves

1. Remove the giblets and neck from the turkey, wash and pat dry.

2. Fry the crumbled sausage with 2 tablespoons of butter or olive oil in a large skillet until lightly browned. Remove the sausage and leave behind any butter or oil. Fry the vegetables for 5 minutes over medium heat.

3. Place the sausage, vegetables, garlic, apple, parsley, bread crumbs, salt, pepper, and half of the thyme leaves in a large mixing bowl. Stir to blend well.

4. Stuff the turkey with the dressing and truss it for baking. Rub the remaining thyme leaves and butter or oil over the outside of the bird. Place a small piece of foil over the breast of the bird. Bake in a 350°F oven for 15 to 20 minutes per pound until done. Don't overcook. Remove the foil for the last half-hour and baste frequently. Let the bird rest for 15 minutes. Remove the dressing, carve, and serve.

CHICKEN BREASTS AND
VEGETABLES BAKED IN FOIL

> *4 12-inch squares of heavy-duty aluminum foil*
> *4 skinless, boneless chicken breast halves, between*
>   *1 and 1½ pounds total weight*
> *1 medium carrot, peeled and julienne sliced*
> *1 small turnip or parsnip, peeled and julienne sliced*
> *2 shallots or 1 small red onion, thinly sliced*
> *Salt and pepper to taste*
> *1 tablespoon fresh or 1 teaspoon dried thyme or*
>   *tarragon leaves*
> *8 tablespoons heavy cream*

1. Lay a sheet of aluminum foil on a work surface in front of you. Place a chicken breast in the center.

2. Toss the carrot and turnip into a pot of boiling water and cook for 1 minute. Drain and cool.

3. Sprinkle a quarter of the carrot and turnip, plus a quarter of the shallots, over the chicken breast. Season with salt, pepper, and herbs. Drizzle 2 tablespoons of cream on the breast.

4. Fold the aluminum to make a tightly sealed packet. Repeat with remaining breasts.

5. Bake in a 375°F oven for 20 minutes. Remove from the packet and serve, pouring remaining cream over the top.

FISH IN FOIL WITH
ASIAN ROOT SPICES

> *4 12-inch sheets of heavy-duty aluminum foil*
> *4 fillets or steaks of firm-fleshed fish such as cod,*
>   *scrod, haddock, snapper, grouper, or salmon*
> *1 cup shredded daikon radish*
> *1 cup shredded sweet potato*
> *½ cup minced scallions, tops included*

1 teaspoon grated fresh ginger
1 tablespoon Asian sesame seed oil
2 tablespoons soy sauce

1. Lay a sheet of aluminum foil on a work surface in front of you. Place a piece of fish in the center.

2. Sprinkle a quarter of the daikon, sweet potato, scallions, and ginger over the fish. Mix the sesame oil with the soy sauce and sprinkle a little on the fish.

3. Repeat with remaining foil, fish, and other ingredients. Bake the fish in a 375°F oven for 20 minutes. Remove fish from the packet and top with remaining juices.

MEAT AND POTATOES SHISH KEBAB

1 boneless pork or beef tenderloin or other tender
    meat
8 to 10 small red or white new potatoes
3 large sweet onions such as Vidalia or Walla Walla
¾ cup olive or other vegetable oil
3 tablespoons red wine vinegar
1 teaspoon Dijon mustard
Salt and pepper to taste
1 teaspoon minced herbs such as chives, parsley,
    rosemary, or thyme

1. Slice the meat into 1-inch-square chunks. Cut the potatoes into ¾-inch-thick rounds or wedges. Cut the onions into ¾-inch wedges.

2. Make the basting sauce by whisking together the oil, vinegar, mustard, salt, pepper, and herbs.

3. Thread the meat, potatoes, and onions on skewers. Brush with the basting sauce and barbecue on the grill outside or in the broiler in the oven for 10 to 12 minutes. Baste frequently.

PORK CHOPS BRAISED WITH PARSNIPS

1 tablespoon vegetable oil
¼ cup all-purpose flour
½ teaspoon each salt, pepper, and paprika
4 1-inch-thick center-cut pork chops
1 pound parsnips
1 cup water
1 teaspoon flour
1 tablespoon brown grainy mustard
1½ cups milk

1. Warm the oil in a large, heavy skillet with a tight-fitting lid over medium heat for 1 minute.

2. Place the flour, salt, pepper, and paprika in a medium mixing bowl. Stir to blend well. Dredge the pork chops in the seasoned flour and place in the skillet.

3. Fry the pork chops for 5 minutes, turn, and fry the other side for 3 minutes, until golden brown.

4. Peel and slice the parsnips lengthwise into quarters. Cut the quarters crosswise into ½-inch chunks. Add the parsnips to the pork chops. Pour in the water, cover the skillet, and reduce the heat to medium-low. Simmer for 30 minutes.

5. Remove the pork chops from the skillet. Add the flour and mustard and stir. Add the milk and stir to form a creamy white gravy. Place the pork chops on a platter and pour the gravy with the parsnips over the chops.

POT-AU-FEU

Pot-au-feu literally means pot on the fire. It is a favorite French family dinner of beef and vegetables simmered together. The rich cooking broth is served as a first-course soup, followed by the sliced meats and vegetables.

> 1 beef bone or veal knuckle for soup, cracked by the butcher
> 1 3-pound piece of beef brisket (do not use corned beef)
> 3 quarts cold water
> 1 teaspoon salt
> 5 carrots, peeled and cut in chunks
> 2 turnips, peeled and cut in chunks
> 4 leeks, white part only, chopped
> 1 large onion, sliced
> 1 herb bouquet made of 3 sprigs parsley, 1 sprig fresh thyme, and a bay leaf tied together. If you can't make an herb bouquet, simply add the herbs and strain them out later.
> 1 medium onion stuck with 2 whole cloves
> Salt and pepper to taste

1. Place the soup bones and brisket in a soup pot just large enough to hold them. Cover with water and salt. Bring the water to a simmer and skim off the scum that rises to the top.

2. Cover and slowly boil the meat for 3 hours. Add the vegetables and the herb bouquet and the onion stuck with the clove. Add salt and pepper. Simmer for an additional hour.

3. Remove the meat and vegetables to a heated platter and keep warm. Strain out the herb bouquet or loose herbs and the onion with cloves and discard.

4. Ladle the broth into soup bowls and serve with toasted French bread and butter.

5. Slice the meat and vegetables and serve with mayonnaise or mustard.

COQ AU RIESLING

French coq au vin, chicken in wine sauce, is usually made with red wine. But this version is made with the fruity white wine from the

Germanic part of France called Alsace.

> 1 whole chicken cut up for frying or 6 to 8 chicken
>   thighs or legs
> ½ cup all-purpose flour
> ½ teaspoon each salt and pepper
> 3 tablespoons butter or vegetable oil
> 1½ cups dry Riesling wine
> 2 shallots or 1 medium onion, peeled and chopped
> 10 large mushrooms, wiped clean and sliced
> 3 turnips, cut in wedges
> 3 carrots, peeled and cut in wedges
> 1 small celery root, peeled and cut in wedges
> 1½ cups chicken broth or stock
> Salt and pepper to taste
> 1 tablespoon minced fresh tarragon, thyme, or sum-
>   mer savory

1. Place the chicken, flour, salt, and pepper in a large mixing bowl. Dredge the chicken in the seasoned flour and shake off any excess.

2. Fry the chicken pieces in the butter in a large skillet until lightly browned all over, about 10 minutes.

3. Remove the chicken to a casserole or baking dish. Pour the wine into the frying pan and deglaze the pan. Surround the chicken with the vegetables and add the wine, stock, salt, pepper, and herbs.

4. Cover and bake in a 350°F oven 30 to 40 minutes.

ITALIAN SAUSAGE WITH
PARSNIPS AND TOMATOES

> 4 to 6 sweet Italian sausages, about 1 pound
> 1 pound parsnips, peeled and cut into ¼-inch-thick
>   rings
> 1 medium onion, chopped
> 3 cloves garlic, minced

1 medium green or red pepper, chopped
2 tablespoons flat leaf parsley, minced
1 tablespoon fresh or 1 teaspoon dried oregano
1 tablespoon fresh or 1 teaspoon dried basil
1 28-ounce can whole or crushed tomatoes
Salt and pepper to taste

1. Sauté the sausages in a large skillet over medium heat for 15 minutes. Turn often to make them browned all over. Add the parsnips and stir to coat with the rendered sausage fat.

2. Add the onions, garlic, pepper, parsley, oregano, basil, tomatoes, salt, and pepper. Cover the skillet and simmer for 30 minutes.

ROAST DUCK WITH TURNIPS

2 ducks
16 to 20 very small baby turnips or 4 to 6 medium-
    sized ones
Salt and pepper to taste
¼ cup brandy or port wine
2 tablespoons butter
2 tablespoons all-purpose flour

1. Preheat the oven to 400°F.

2. Truss the ducks and place them on a rack in a roasting pan. Cover each duck breast with a small sheet of aluminum foil. Pour ½ cup of water into the pan and place the pan in the oven. Bake for 45 minutes.

3. Meanwhile, peel the tiny turnips and place them in a pan of water. If you have larger turnips, peel them, cut them in eighths, and place them in a pan of water. Boil the turnips for 5 minutes. Drain and reserve.

4. After 45 minutes, take the ducks from the oven. Drain off all but 2 tablespoons of the fat and juices. Scatter the turnips under the

ducks, remove the aluminum foil, and bake for another 15 minutes.

5. Remove the ducks from the oven and test. The leg should move freely and the juices run clear when you pierce the bird's thigh with a fork.

6. Place the ducks on a platter, cover loosely with foil, and keep warm. Remove the turnips and keep warm.

7. Remove the rack and place the roasting pan directly on the stove. Skim the fat from the juice. Add salt, pepper, and brandy to the remaining juices in the pan. Pour in ½ cup water. Bring to the boil, scraping the pan to get any brown bits. Mix the butter with the flour and add to the juices, stirring to form a gravy. Carve the ducks and serve with turnips and gravy.

SWEDISH MEATBALLS WITH RUTABAGA

1 large rutabaga
½ pound ground pork
½ pound ground veal
1 teaspoon salt
½ teaspoon pepper
¼ teaspoon mace or nutmeg
3 tablespoons all-purpose flour
1 egg
½ cup cream, half-and-half, or milk
4 tablespoons butter
3 cups beef stock or broth

1. Peel the rutabaga and cut into 1-inch chunks. Place in a sauce-pan, cover with water, and boil for 10 minutes. Drain.

2. In a large mixing bowl, blend the pork, veal, salt, pepper, mace, 1 tablespoon flour, egg, and cream. Form the mixture into 1-inch meatballs.

3. Melt 1 tablespoon butter in a frying pan and sauté the meatballs

in batches until browned all over. Remove the meatballs from the pan. Add the remaining butter and flour and stir to form a paste. Add the beef broth and stir to form a creamy sauce.

4. Place the meatballs and the rutabaga in a casserole. Pour the sauce over all and bake in a 350°F oven for 30 minutes. Serve on a buffet or as a satisfying dinner with noodles.

NEW ENGLAND BOILED DINNER

1 4- to 5-pound corned beef brisket
1 teaspoon dried basil
1 bay leaf
8 carrots, peeled and chopped in thirds
4 parsnips, peeled and chopped in thirds
6 turnips, peeled and quartered
8 potatoes, peeled and quartered
1 small head cabbage, cut into sixths

1. Cover the beef with cold water and add the basil and the bay leaf. Bring to a boil, reduce the heat, and simmer 3 to 4 hours.

2. About 30 minutes before serving, add all the vegetables except the cabbage. (If you have an aversion to pink, you may want to boil the beets separately.) Fifteen minutes before serving, add the cabbage. Continue simmering till all the meat and vegetables are tender.

3. The traditional way to serve New England Boiled Dinner is to place the sliced beef in the center of a large platter and surround it with the vegetables. Serve pickles and horseradish on the side. Everything that is left over is chopped and made into red flannel hash, but that's another recipe.

ROOTS POT ROAST

3½- to 4-pound chuck roast
3 tablespoons flour
1 teaspoon each salt and pepper
1 rutabaga, peeled and cut in 1-inch chunks
2 onions, peeled and quartered
4 parsnips, peeled and left whole
2 tablespoons flour
2 tablespoons butter

1. Preheat the oven to 325°F.

2. Place the roast on a large sheet of waxed paper. Rub it all over with the flour, salt, and pepper.

3. Place the roast in a large roasting pan. Surround with the rutabaga, onions, and parsnips. Cover with water and cover with a lid or aluminum foil. Roast the meat for 3 to 3½ hours or until tender.

4. Remove the meat and vegetables from the pan. Place the pan over a burner and cook, stirring to pick up any browned bits. Using the back of a fork, blend the flour and butter in a mixing cup and then add to the pan juices. Stir and cook to form a smooth gravy.

ROAST FRESH HAM WITH PARSNIPS AND BEETS

1 whole fresh ham, about 8 pounds
3 cloves garlic, cut into slivers
2 tablespoons fresh, or 2 teaspoons dried, minced
  thyme
Salt and black pepper to taste
¼ cup olive oil
6 large parsnips, peeled
6 large beets, washed but unpeeled

3 tablespoons all-purpose flour
2 cups water

1. Preheat the oven to 325°F.

2. Cut several tiny pockets in the ham and insert a sliver of garlic in each. Sprinkle the thyme, salt, pepper, and olive oil over the ham and rub them in with your hands.

3. Place the ham in a roasting pan and arrange the vegetables around. Bake the ham for 4 hours.

4. Remove the ham and the vegetables from the roasting pan and cover with foil to keep warm. Spoon the fat from the pan, leaving the juices behind. Place the pan on a stovetop burner over medium heat and sprinkle with flour. Stir to form a creamy paste. Add the water and stir to form a creamy gravy.

5. Slice enough pieces of ham for your guests. Peel the beets and cut into wedges. Cut the parsnips into pieces. Place them all on a serving platter and serve the gravy on the side.

NINE

Roots with Grains, Noodles, and Pastas

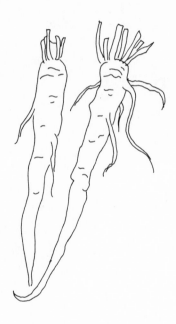

People don't always think of serving root vegetables in fried rice, in pasta or macaroni dishes, or in Asian stir-fries. But if you are looking for ways to reduce your meat intake in these dishes, roots are an ideal substitute. They have a firmer texture than many other vegetables and they have an earthy flavor that gives people a taste impression that they are eating as much meat as they want. Furthermore, mixing root vegetables with grains is a great way to increase your intake of complex carbohydrates.

This chapter has grain dishes with roots from many cultures: Asian, Scandinavian, German, Polish, North African, Italian, Eastern European Jewish, Louisiana Cajun, and even American suburban.

All of the recipes in this chapter will yield 4 to 6 servings.

ROOTS FRIED RICE

> 1 tablespoon vegetable oil
> 1 medium onion, peeled and sliced fine
> 1 teaspoon minced fresh ginger
> 1 clove garlic, peeled and minced
> 1 carrot, peeled and grated
> 1 cup grated daikon radish
> 2 cups cold cooked rice
> 1 cup chopped cooked chicken, pork, or shrimp
> 2 tablespoons soy sauce
> ¼ cup broth or water

1. Heat the oil in a large, heavy skillet over medium heat for 1 minute. Add the onion, ginger, garlic, carrot, and daikon radish and sauté for 5 minutes, stirring often.

2. Add the cooked rice, chicken, soy sauce, and broth. Fry for 2

to 3 minutes, stirring constantly, until rice is heated through. Serve with extra soy sauce.

NORTH AFRICAN COUSCOUS

> *1 tablespoon olive or other vegetable oil*
> *½ pound ground lamb, beef, chicken, or turkey*
> *1 medium onion, peeled and chopped*
> *4 medium cloves garlic, peeled and chopped*
> *2 medium carrots, peeled and chopped*
> *2 medium turnips, chopped*
> *1 16-ounce can garbanzo beans, drained*
> *¼ teaspoon each ground cumin and cinnamon*
> *2 cups beef broth or stock*
> *Salt and pepper to taste*
> *1 cup couscous*
> *1 cup warm water*

1. Heat the oil in a medium soup pot over medium heat for 1 minute. Add the meat and sauté for 3 minutes, stirring occasionally. Add the onion, garlic, carrots, and turnips. Stir to coat with oil.

2. Add the garbanzo beans, cumin, cinnamon, broth, salt, and pepper. Cover and simmer for 30 minutes.

3. Place the couscous in a medium mixing bowl. Add the warm water and let stand for 5 to 10 minutes. Stir to fluff the grains.

4. Place a large spoonful of couscous in individual soup bowls. Spoon the meat and vegetables over the grain. Ladle on some sauce and serve remaining sauce on the side.

FUSILLI PASTA WITH
ITALIAN SAUSAGES AND CELERIAC

> *¾ pound fresh sweet Italian sausages*
> *1 medium-sized celeriac, peeled, chopped small,*
> *   and steamed*

2 tablespoons fruity olive oil
2 tablespoons unsalted butter
3 tablespoons fresh minced parsley
½ cup dry white wine, chicken stock, or water
1 pound fusilli pasta, boiled and drained
1 cup grated aged provolone cheese
Salt and freshly ground black pepper to taste

1. Sauté the Italian sausages in a large frying pan over low heat for 15 minutes. Remove them from the pan, drain off the fat, and slice the sausages into thick rounds.

2. Return the sausage pieces to the pan, along with the cooked celeriac, the olive oil, and the butter. Add the parsley. Sauté over high heat for 1 minute. Add the liquid and sauté another minute. Add the drained pasta and stir all the ingredients together and heat thoroughly.

3. Spoon the mixture into warmed pasta bowls and sprinkle with the cheese, salt, and pepper.

YELLOW POTATOES AND VEAL IN A HORSERADISH CREAM SAUCE ON KLUSKI NOODLES

2 tablespoons butter or vegetable oil
2 medium yellow Finnish or Yukon Gold potatoes,
  peeled and diced
½ pound ground veal
½ cup beef or chicken broth
2 tablespoons all-purpose flour
2½ cups whole milk or half-and-half
½ cup minced fresh parsley
2 tablespoons freshly grated or prepared horse-
  radish
Salt and pepper to taste
¾ pound Kluski noodles

1. Heat the butter or oil in a medium soup pot over medium heat for 1 minute. Add the potatoes and veal and sauté for 3 to 5 minutes, stirring occasionally.

2. Add the beef or chicken broth, reduce the heat to medium-low, cover, and simmer for 10 minutes.

3. Add the flour and stir to form a creamy paste. Add the milk and stir to form a creamy gravy. Add the parsley, horseradish, salt, and pepper. Cover and keep the heat on low while you prepare the noodles.

4. Cook the Kluski noodles in boiling water until soft. Drain. Toss the Kluski noodles with the stew and serve.

CREAMY CELERIAC WITH HAM AND MUSHROOMS ON SPINACH NOODLES

1 medium celeriac
1 tablespoon butter
1 cup diced smoked ham
1 cup chopped mushrooms
2 cups heavy cream
Salt and pepper to taste
¾ pound spinach noodles

1. Peel the celeriac and chop it into small diced pieces. Place the pieces in a saucepan, cover with water, and bring to a boil. Reduce heat to medium and simmer for 10 minutes. Drain.

2. Melt the butter in a large skillet over medium heat. Add the celeriac, ham, and mushrooms and sauté for 5 minutes. Add the cream, salt, and pepper, and cook until the cream thickens and you get a creamy gravy.

3. Boil the noodles in plenty of water 8 to 10 minutes or until al dente. Drain and reserve.

4. Place the noodles in a large pasta bowl. Pour the sauce over, toss, and serve.

KASHA VARNISHKES WITH PARSNIPS

1 cup kasha
1½ cups boiling water
1 cup bow tie noodles
3 tablespoons vegetable oil
1 medium onion, peeled and chopped
3 parsnips, peeled and slivered
2 eggs, well beaten
Salt and pepper to taste

1. Place the kasha in a medium heat-resistant mixing bowl. Pour the hot water over and let rest. Stir occasionally and lightly with a fork to let the kasha fluff up. Reserve.

2. Boil the bow tie noodles in plenty of water 8 to 10 minutes or until al dente. Drain and reserve.

3. In a large skillet, heat the oil over medium heat for 1 minute. Add the chopped onion and parsnips. Sauté for 5 minutes. Add the beaten eggs and scramble them.

4. Add the kasha, the bow ties, the salt and pepper, and stir to blend well. Add an additional tablespoon of oil and up to ¼ cup water if the mixture is too dry.

GERMAN SPAETZLE WITH PORK
AND HAMBURG PARSLEY

1 package German spaetzle, available in packaged
*   noodle and rice sections of many grocery stores*
2 tablespoons butter or vegetable oil
¾ pound ground pork
3 medium Hamburg parsley roots or 1 large celery
*   root*
2 tablespoons all-purpose flour
2½ cups beef or chicken broth
1 teaspoon caraway seeds
Salt and pepper to taste

1. Cook the spaetzle (tiny German dumplings) according to package instructions. Drain and keep warm. (In a pinch, you could substitute plain potato pierogi.)

2. Heat the butter or oil in a medium soup pot over medium heat. Add the pork and parsley or celery root. Sauté for 5 minutes, stirring often.

3. Sprinkle the flour over the meat and vegetables and stir. Add the broth and stir. Add the caraway seeds, salt, and pepper, reduce the heat to low, and simmer for 15 minutes, stirring occasionally.

4. Ladle the stew over the spaetzle or pierogi and serve.

STIR-FRIED PARSNIPS WITH CHINESE VEGETABLES

1 pound parsnips
2 tablespoons vegetable oil
1 tablespoon fresh minced ginger
2 stalks Chinese or 1 stalk American broccoli,
*   chopped*
2 cups chopped bok choy cabbage
3 scallions, sliced thin, green parts included
2 ounces dried Chinese mushrooms, soaked in hot
*   water, or substitute 1 cup sliced fresh button*
*   mushrooms*
1 tablespoon soy sauce
1 teaspoon sesame sauce
1 tablespoon cornstarch blended with 1 cup cold
*   water*

1. Peel the parsnips and cut on the bias into angled circles.

2. Heat a wok or large skillet over medium-high heat for 1 minute. Place the oil in the wok and stir to coat the sides. Add the parsnips, ginger, and broccoli. Stir-fry for 1 minute.

3. Add the bok choy, scallions, and mushrooms and stir-fry for 2 minutes. Add the soy sauce, sesame oil, and the cornstarch water. Stir to form a creamy gravy. Serve with white rice.

SPAGHETTI WITH CARROTS AND ZUCCHINI

¾ pound spaghetti
½ pound carrots
½ pound zucchini
3 tablespoons butter
3 tablespoons olive oil
1 small red onion, minced
2 cloves garlic, minced
Salt and pepper to taste
2 tablespoons fresh minced parsley
Grated Romano or Parmesan cheese

1. Boil the spaghetti in plenty of water for 8 minutes or until al dente. Drain and keep warm.

2. Peel and grate the carrots. Grate the zucchini. Combine the two and reserve.

3. Heat the butter and oil in a large skillet over medium-high heat for 1 minute. Add the carrots, zucchini, onion, and garlic and sauté for 3 to 5 minutes or until the carrot is tender.

4. Add the salt, pepper, and parsley and stir. Pour the carrot sauce over the spaghetti and toss to blend well. Serve with grated cheese.

MACARONI AND CHEESE WITH SWEET POTATO AND TUNA

¾ pound elbow or ribbon macaroni
3 tablespoons butter
3 tablespoons all-purpose flour
3 cups milk
1 pound sweet potatoes, peeled and grated
1 6½-ounce can tuna in water or oil, drained
2 cups mild Cheddar, Colby, or longhorn cheese, grated
Salt and pepper to taste

1. Preheat the oven to 350°F.

2. Boil the macaroni in plenty of water 6 to 8 minutes or until al dente. Drain and keep warm.

3. Melt the butter in a 2-quart saucepan and add the flour. Stir to form a creamy paste. Add the milk and whisk to break up any lumps. Stir and cook over medium heat to form a creamy sauce.

4. In a large mixing bowl, blend together the macaroni and sweet potato with the cream sauce, tuna, cheese, salt, and pepper. Spoon into a casserole dish and bake in the oven 15 to 20 minutes or until bubbly.

CAJUN TURNIPS WITH SMOKED HAM JAMBALAYA

> 2 tablespoons olive or other vegetable oil
> ½ cup onion, chopped fine
> 3 cloves garlic, minced
> ½ cup finely chopped celery
> 2 medium turnips
> 1 cup chopped smoked ham or kielbasy
> 1 cup white or brown rice
> ½ teaspoon each salt, black pepper, and cayenne
>   pepper
> 1 teaspoon dried thyme
> 2 cups water (2½ cups water if using brown rice)

1. Heat the olive oil in a large pot—a Dutch oven is perfect—for 1 minute over medium-high heat. Add the onion, garlic, celery, turnips, and ham. Sauté, stirring often, for 3 minutes.

2. Add the rice, salt, black and cayenne pepper, and thyme. Stir and sauté for another 2 minutes. Add the water, bring the mixture to the boil, cover, turn the heat to low, and simmer for 15 minutes for white rice, 30 minutes for brown.

3. Check for doneness. If the rice is tender and the water is gone, turn off the heat and let rest 10 minutes. If the rice is still a little firm,

add ¼ cup water and continue cooking. Stir the jambalaya and serve. Pass hot sauce on the side.

STIR-FRIED BEEF WITH TURNIPS

> *2 tablespoons vegetable oil*
> *1 pound boneless sirloin steak, sliced very thin*
>   *across the grain*
> *2 medium turnips, peeled and sliced*
> *1 medium red or green bell pepper, sliced thin*
> *1 medium onion, sliced thin*
> *1 clove garlic, minced*
> *1 tablespoon fresh, or ½ teaspoon dried, minced*
>   *ginger*
> *2 tablespoons soy sauce*
> *1 tablespoon cornstarch*
> *1 cup water*

1. Heat a wok or large skillet over medium-high heat for 1 minute. Add 1 tablespoon oil and stir to coat the sides of the pan. Add the beef and stir-fry for 1 minute. Remove and keep warm.

2. Add the other tablespoon of vegetable oil and stir. Add the turnips, pepper, onion, garlic, and ginger. Stir-fry for 3 minutes.

3. Return the beef to the pan along with the soy sauce. Stir the cornstarch with the water, making sure to break up any lumps. Pour the water over the meat and vegetables, reduce the heat to low, and stir until a creamy gravy forms.

SCANDINAVIAN RUTABAGA WITH SALMON AND DILL

2 small, fist-size rutabagas, peeled and cubed
¼ pound Norwegian or any good-quality smoked salmon
1 cup sour cream
¼ cup milk
1 tablespoon fresh minced dill or 1 teaspoon dried
1 pound thick-cut egg noodles
½ teaspoon each salt and freshly ground black pepper

1. Steam the rutabaga till tender, about 15 minutes. Drain and keep warm. Slice the smoked salmon into small matchstick-thin pieces. Put the rutabaga, smoked salmon, sour cream, milk, and dill in the top of a double boiler and heat till piping hot. Stir frequently.

2. Boil and drain the noodles. Serve the rutabaga and salmon over the warm noodles. Sprinkle with salt and pepper.

ROOTS RISOTTO

3 tablespoons butter
3 tablespoons olive oil
1 large red onion, minced
2 cups short-grain Arborio rice
4 cups chicken broth or stock, heated
½ cup each slivered carrot, parsnip, and celeriac
⅓ cup Parmesan cheese
Salt and pepper to taste

1. Heat the butter and oil over medium heat in a large skillet or pan. Add the minced onion and sauté for 3 to 5 minutes.

2. Add the rice to the onion and sauté for 5 minutes, stirring often. Pour in ½ cup warm chicken broth and cook, stirring constantly until broth is absorbed.

3. Add the carrot, parsnip, and celeriac and another ½ cup broth. Cook and stir until broth is absorbed. Keep adding the broth in ½-cup portions and stirring until rice is creamy and all the broth is gone.

4. Remove the risotto from the heat and stir in the cheese. Salt and pepper to taste. Let rest 5 minutes, covered, and serve.

ROOTS RAVIOLI WITH A LIGHT BUTTER SAUCE

2 medium beets
1 egg
8 ounces fresh ricotta cheese
⅛ teaspoon nutmeg
Salt and pepper to taste
1 package prepared ravioli wrappers
1 stick unsalted butter
2 tablespoons fresh minced parsley

1. Trim the tops off the beets and wash. Boil them in water until very tender, about 20 minutes. Drain and peel. Purée in a food processor until very creamy.

2. Place the beets in a medium mixing bowl. Add the egg, ricotta cheese, nutmeg, salt, and pepper. Stir to blend well.

3. Place a small spoonful of beet mixture in the center of a ravioli wrapper. Moisten the edges of the skin with water and place another wrapper on top. Crimp the edges with a fork to make a ravioli. Make the rest the same way.

4. Bring 2 quarts of water to a light boil and cook the ravioli a few at a time until they float and puff a little, only about 2 to 3 minutes. Drain and keep warm.

5. Melt the butter in a small saucepan.

6. Place the ravioli in wide, flat soup bowls, pour butter over them, sprinkle with parsley, and serve. Pass grated cheese if you like.

TEN

The Sweetest Roots of All

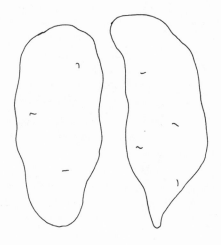

R oots for dessert may sound a little off the wall, but not so much when you stop to think about it. Carrot cake is now widely popular after its rebirth as a health food in the 1960s. It is still a healthy food, but now people realize that it is delicious, so delicious, in fact, that this chapter will feature not one but two carrot cake recipes.

Another way to see that roots can be made into delicious desserts is to think about America's favorite holiday pie, made from the lowly and seemingly improbable pumpkin. Nobody questions that pumpkin makes a tasty pie, and nobody will question that parsnips make a delicious pie, too, after trying the one in this chapter.

It makes sense that sweet potatoes will make good desserts, even though if you peel a sweet potato and eat it raw, it doesn't exactly taste sweet like an apple or a pear. This chapter will feature sweet potato pie and sweet potato doughnuts.

Finally, there is ginger, which should not surprise anyone who is used to eating gingerbread and gingersnap cookies. But most people are looking at powdered ginger out of a can. These recipes will feature fresh ginger as well as the aromatic powdered variety.

CLASSIC CARROT CAKE

NOTE: Grated parsnips can be substituted for grated carrots to make a delicious classic parsnip cake.

> *1½ cups sifted all-purpose white flour*
> *1 teaspoon baking soda*
> *1 teaspoon baking powder*
> *½ teaspoon salt*
> *1 teaspoon cinnamon*
> *½ teaspoon ground cloves*
> *½ teaspoon ground nutmeg or mace*
> *2 eggs*
> *¾ cup vegetable oil*
> *1 cup sugar*
> *1½ cups grated carrots*

1. Preheat the oven to 350°F. Grease and flour an 8-inch-square cake pan.

2. In a large bowl, place the sifted flour, baking soda, baking powder, salt, cinnamon, cloves, and nutmeg. Stir to blend well.

3. In a separate bowl, beat the eggs with a fork for 30 seconds. Add the vegetable oil, sugar, and grated carrots. Stir to blend well.

4. Add the wet ingredients to the dry ones and stir. Pour the mixture into the cake pan and bake in the oven for 45 minutes or until golden brown and a toothpick inserted in the center comes out clean.

5. Remove from the oven and let cool.

HAWAIIAN CARROT CAKE

> *1 large orange, peeled*
> *2 cups unsifted flour*
> *2 cups sugar*
> *2 teaspoons baking powder*

2 teaspoons baking soda
2 teaspoons cinnamon
2 teaspoons nutmeg
1 teaspoon salt
1¼ cups salad oil
4 eggs
2 cups grated carrots
½ cup nuts
Confectioner's sugar

1. Cut orange into 8 wedges, then into 3 or 4 pieces. Purée in blender.

2. In a large mixing bowl, stir together the flour, sugar, baking powder, baking soda, cinnamon, nutmeg, and salt.

3. Add the oil, orange purée, and eggs. Mix thoroughly.

4. Blend in carrots and nuts.

5. Pour into greased and floured baking pan, 8 inches by 10 inches.

6. Bake at 350°F for 1 hour or until done.

7. Dust with confectioner's sugar before serving.

PARSNIP WALNUT CAKE

1¼ cups sifted whole wheat flour
1 teaspoon each baking powder and baking soda
½ teaspoon salt
1 teaspoon ground cinnamon
½ teaspoon each allspice and mace
½ cup ground walnuts, hazelnuts, pecans, or sun-
*   flower seeds*
2 eggs
½ cup honey
¾ cup vegetable oil
¼ cup low-fat plain yogurt
1½ cups grated parsnips

1. Preheat the oven to 350°F. Grease and flour an 8-inch cake pan.

2. In a large mixing bowl, mix together the flour, baking powder and soda, salt, cinnamon, allspice, and mace. Stir to blend well.

3. In a separate bowl, mix together the nuts, eggs, honey, oil, yogurt, and parsnips. Stir to blend well.

4. Stir the wet ingredients into the dry. Pour into the cake pan and bake for 45 minutes or until a toothpick inserted into the cake comes out clean.

5. Cool and serve.

GINGERBREAD

    2 cups sifted all-purpose white flour
    1 teaspoon baking soda
    ¼ teaspoon salt
    1 teaspoon ground ginger
    ½ teaspoon freshly grated ginger
    1 teaspoon cinnamon
    2 eggs
    ½ cup firmly packed light brown sugar
    ½ cup molasses
    1 cup buttermilk
    ½ cup vegetable oil

1. Preheat the oven to 350°F. Grease and flour an 8- or 9-inch square cake pan.

2. In a large mixing bowl, blend together the sifted flour, baking soda, salt, ginger, and cinnamon.

3. In a separate bowl, mix together the eggs, sugar, molasses, buttermilk, and vegetable oil. Add the wet ingredients to the dry ingredients and stir.

4. Pour the batter into the cake pan and bake for 1 hour.

SWEET POTATO PECAN PIE

FOR THE PIE CRUST

Make your favorite pie crust, buy a ready-made pie
   crust at the supermarket, or follow this recipe.
1½ cups sifted all-purpose white flour
½ teaspoon salt
½ cup butter, margarine, or vegetable shortening
3 tablespoons cold water

Mix together the flour and the salt. Add the butter and stir with a
fork, cutting the butter into the flour to form a crumbly, granular
mixture. Add the water and stir to form a ball. Roll the dough out
and fit it into a 9-inch pie plate.

FOR THE FILLING

1 cup mashed sweet potatoes
½ cup light or dark brown sugar
¾ teaspoon cinnamon
¼ teaspoon each powdered ginger and cloves
¾ cup scalded milk
2 eggs

Mix together all the ingredients and pour the mixture into the pie
shell. Bake at 375°F for 20 minutes. Remove from the oven.

FOR THE TOPPING

¼ cup butter or margarine, at room temperature
½ cup brown sugar
¾ cup pecan halves or chopped pecans

Mix the topping ingredients together and sprinkle them on the pie
filling. Return the pie to the oven and bake an additional 25 minutes.
Remove and cool.

SWEET POTATO DOUGHNUTS

> *3 cups sifted all-purpose white flour*
> *4 teaspoons baking powder*
> *1 teaspoon salt*
> *½ teaspoon each nutmeg and cinnamon*
> *2 eggs*
> *1 cup white or light brown sugar*
> *1 cup mashed sweet potatoes*
> *2 tablespoons vegetable oil*
> *1 cup milk*
> *1 quart vegetable oil for frying*
> *Powdered sugar*

1. In a large mixing bowl, sift together and mix the flour, baking powder, salt, nutmeg, and cinnamon.

2. In a separate mixing bowl, beat the eggs. Add the sugar, mashed potatoes, vegetable oil, and milk. Stir to blend well. Add the wet ingredients to the dry and stir.

3. Stir the ingredients together and turn out on to a floured surface. Roll the dough to a thickness of ¼ inch. Cut into doughnut shapes, or any shape you like.

4. Heat the oil to 360°F to 370°F in a large, deep-sided pot. Fry the doughnuts for 2 to 3 minutes or until lightly browned. Drain and dust with powdered sugar. Makes approximately 24 doughnuts.

PARSNIP PIE

Make your own favorite pie crust, buy one from the supermarket, or follow the pie crust recipe in the previous recipe, for Sweet Potato Pecan Pie.

> *1¾ cups mashed cooked parsnips*
> *1 teaspoon salt*
> *1½ cups milk*

2 large eggs
1 cup sugar
1 teaspoon cinnamon
½ teaspoon each nutmeg and powdered ginger
1 tablespoon butter

1. Preheat the oven to 425°F. Line a pie plate with pie crust.

2. In a medium mixing bowl, mix together all the ingredients. Pour into the pie shell and bake for 45 to 55 minutes. Cool and serve.

GINGERSNAP COOKIES

1 cup butter, margarine, or vegetable shortening
1 cup sugar
2 eggs
½ cup molasses
4½ cups sifted all-purpose white flour
1½ teaspoons powdered ginger
1½ teaspoons minced fresh ginger
1 teaspoon baking soda
1 teaspoon salt

1. Preheat the oven to 400°F.

2. Whip together the butter and sugar. Add the eggs and molasses and stir to blend well.

3. In a separate bowl, blend together the flour, ginger, baking soda, and salt. Add the wet ingredients to the dry ingredients and stir to blend well.

4. Place teaspoon-sized amounts of cookie batter on a cookie sheet and bake in the oven for 8 to 10 minutes. Repeat until all dough is baked. Cool and serve.

CARROT COOKIES

2 cups sifted all-purpose flour
2 teaspoons baking powder
¼ teaspoon baking soda
¼ teaspoon salt
½ teaspoon cinnamon
½ teaspoon nutmeg
2 cups oatmeal
1 cup raisins
1 cup chopped walnuts or pecans
½ cup butter or margarine
1 cup grated raw carrots
1 cup honey
2 eggs, well beaten

1. Preheat the oven to 350°F. Grease a baking sheet.

2. In a large mixing bowl, mix the flour, baking powder, baking soda, salt, and spices. Stir in the oatmeal, raisins, and nuts. Blend well.

3. In a separate mixing bowl, cream the butter or margarine by whipping it to a creamy paste. Add the carrots and stir, then add the honey and eggs. Stir carefully to blend well.

4. Add the dry mixture to the wet mixture and stir to blend well. Drop by the teaspoonful onto the baking sheet and bake for 25 to 30 minutes. Makes 36 small cookies.

CARROT CUSTARD

1½ cups chopped carrots
1 cup half-and-half
½ cup heavy cream
3 large eggs
¼ teaspoon ground ginger
⅛ teaspoon salt
½ cup sugar

1. Preheat the oven to 325°F.

2. Place the chopped carrots in a saucepan, cover with water, and cook over high heat 8 to 10 minutes or until carrots are tender. Drain carrots, cool slightly, and purée in a food processor.

3. Pour the half-and-half and the heavy cream into a saucepan. Place the pan over medium heat until tiny bubbles form around the edges of the fluid. Don't boil. Remove and let cool.

4. In a medium mixing bowl, whip the eggs and ginger together. Gradually add the scalded cream to the eggs, a tablespoon at a time at first. Stir to blend well. Add the carrot purée, the salt, and the sugar and blend well.

5. Pour the custard mixture into custard cups or ramekins and place them in a pan. Fill the pan with enough water to come halfway up the sides of the cups. Cover with a piece of foil and bake for 40 to 45 minutes or until a knife inserted into the center comes out clean.

6. Remove from oven and take the cups out of the water. Cool. Serves 6.

Index

American crudité platter, 38–41
antipasto, 46–49
apple-carrot-raisin salad, 103

bagna cauda, 47–48
bangers and bashed neeps (English
    sausages and mashed turnips), 146
baskets, 61
batata, *see* boniato
beans
    Italian white bean and vegetable salad,
        111
    minestrone della terra, 84–85
    Oaxacan black bean and vegetable
        salad, 112
    turnip salad with green beans
        viniagrette, 106
    white bean and vegetable soup, 80
beef
    corned beef and parsnip hash, 142–43
    hot Eastern European borscht, 74
    Marie's boiled roots dinner, 153–54
    meat and potatoes shish kebab, 157–58
    Mexican vegetable stew, 148
    New England boiled dinner, 163
    North African couscous, 170
    pot-au-feu, 158–59
    roots pot roast, 164
    stir-fried, with turnips, 177
    Thai, and vegetable salad, 114
    underground soup, 84
    winter roots beef stew, 139–40
beet greens, 10–11
    and beets with bacon vinaigrette, 101
    red and golden beet salad on bed of,
        107
beets, 9–10
    and beet greens with bacon vinaigrette,
        101
    with caraway and oil, 42
    cold beet borscht, 72
    cold beet cups stuffed with herbed
        cheese, 44–45
    hot buttered, 120
    hot Eastern European borscht, 74

mozzarella cheese and, salad, 98
pumpernickel, ham, and pickled beet
    canapé, 52
red and golden beet salad on a bed of
    beet greens, 107
roasted roots with fresh rosemary,
    154–55
roast fresh ham with parsnips and,
    164–65
with sour cream and dill, 100
taboule beet salad, 100–101
warm, in sour cream and horseradish,
    97
with wild rice and hard-cooked eggs,
    99
black radishes with onion, 45
bok choy (Chinese cabbage)
    Asian gingered cole slaw, 108–9
    stir-fried parsnips with Chinese
        vegetables, 174–75
boniato (batata; white sweet potato), 29
    Caribbean, and fruit compote, 135
    Caribbean roots and clam fritters, 66
    French-fried, 58
    Jamaican bouillabaisse, 73–74
borscht
    cold beet, 72
    hot Eastern European, 74
bouillabaisse, Jamaican, 73–74
broccoli, stir-fried parsnips with Chinese
    vegetables, 174–75
bulgur wheat, taboule beet salad, 100–101

cakes
    carrot, classic, 184
    carrot, Hawaiian, 184–85
    gingerbread, 186
    parsnip walnut, 185–86
canapés, 51–53
candied rutabaga, 128–29
carrots, 11–12
    African peanut and, soup, 76
    -apple-raisin salad, 103
    bisque, 74–75
    buttered, rings with lemon, 121

ABOUT THE AUTHOR

Laurence Sombke, a New York–based free-lance writer with an M.A. in journalism, is the author of the cookbook *Fearless Entertaining*. He has written food articles for *New York* magazine, *Esquire*, *Food & Wine*, *USA Today*, *USA Weekend*, and *The Dallas Morning News*, among other publications. In addition, Sombke has been a newswriter for ABC Radio News.

Additional copies of *Glorious Roots: Recipes for Healthy, Tasty Vegetables* may be ordered by sending a check for $19.95 (please add the following for postage and handling: $2.00 for the first copy, $1.00 for each added copy) to:

MasterMedia Limited
17 East 89th Street
New York, NY 10128
(212) 260-5600
(800) 334-8232
(212) 348-2020 (fax)

Laurence Sombke is available for speeches and workshops. Please contact MasterMedia's Speakers' Bureau for availability and fee arrangements. Call Tony Colao at (908) 359-1612.

For interviews, Laurence Sombke can be contacted directly at P.O. Box 354, Claverack, NY 12513; phone: (518) 851-5521.

OTHER MASTERMEDIA BOOKS

THE PREGNANCY AND MOTHERHOOD DIARY: *Planning the First Year of Your Second Career,* by Susan Schiffer Stautberg, is the first and only undated appointment diary that shows how to manage pregnancy and career. ($12.95 spiralbound)

CITIES OF OPPORTUNITY: *Finding the Best Place to Work, Live and Prosper in the 1990's and Beyond,* by Dr. John Tepper Marlin, explores the job and living options for the next decade and into the next century. This consumer guide and handbook, written by one of the world's experts on cities, selects and features forty-six American cities and metropolitan areas. ($13.95 paper, $24.95 cloth)

THE DOLLARS AND SENSE OF DIVORCE: *The Financial Guide for Women,* by Judith Briles, is the first book to combine practical tips on overcoming the legal hurdles with planning before, during and after divorce. ($10.95 paper)

OUT THE ORGANIZATION: *How Fast Could You Find a New Job?,* by Madeleine and Robert Swain, is written for the millions of Americans whose jobs are no longer safe, whose companies are not loyal and who face futures of uncertainty. It gives advice on finding a new job or starting your own business. ($11.95 paper, $17.95 cloth)

AGING PARENTS AND YOU: *A Complete Handbook to Help You Help Your Elders Maintain a Healthy, Productive and Independent Life,* by Eugenia Anderson-Ellis and Marsha Dryan, is a complete guide to providing care to aging relatives. It gives practical advice and resources to the adults who are helping their elders lead productive and independent lives. ($9.95 paper)

CRITICISM IN YOUR LIFE: *How to Give It, How to Take It, How to Make It Work for You,* by Dr. Deborah Bright, offers practical advice, in an upbeat, readable and realistic fashion, for turning criticism into control. Charts and diagrams guide the reader into managing criticism from bosses, spouses, children, friends, neighbors and in-laws. ($9.95 paper, $17.95 cloth)

BEYOND SUCCESS: *How Volunteer Service Can Help You Begin Making a Life Instead of Just a Living,* by John F. Reynolds III and Eleanor Reynolds, C.B.E., is a unique how-to-book targeted to business and professional people considering volunteer work, senior citizens who wish to fill leisure time meaningfully and students trying out various career options. The book is filled with interviews with celebrities, CEOs and average citizens who talk about the benefits of service work. ($9.95 paper, $19.95 cloth)

MANAGING IT ALL: *Time-Saving Ideas for Career, Family, Relationships and Self,* by Beverly Benz Treuille and Susan Schiffer Stautberg, is written for women who are juggling careers and families. Over two hundred career women (ranging from a TV anchorwoman to an investment banker) were interviewed. The book contains many humorous anecdotes on saving time and improving the quality of life for self and family. ($9.95 paper)

REAL LIFE 101: *The Graduate's Guide to Survival,* by Susan Kleinman, supplies welcome advice to those facing "real life" for the first time, focusing on work, money, health and how to deal with freedom and responsibility. ($9.95 paper)

YOUR HEALTHY BODY, YOUR HEALTHY LIFE: *How to Take Control of Your Medical Destiny,* by Donald B. Louria, M.D., provides precise advice and strategies that will help you to live a long and healthy life. Learn also about nutrition, exercise, vitamins and medications, as well as how to control risk factors for major diseases. ($12.95 paper)

THE CONFIDENCE FACTOR: *How Self-Esteem Can Change Your Life,* by Judith Briles, is based on a nationwide survey of six thousand men and women. Briles explores why women so often feel a lack of self-confidence and have a poor opinion of themselves. She offers step-by-step advice on becoming the person you want to be. ($9.95 paper, $18.95 cloth)

THE SOLUTION TO POLLUTION: *101 Things You Can Do to Clean Up Your Environment,* by Laurence Sombke, offers step-by-step techniques on how to conserve more energy, start a recycling center, choose biodegradable products and proceed with individual environmental cleanup projects. ($7.95 paper)

TAKING CONTROL OF YOUR LIFE: *The Secrets of Successful Enterprising Women,* by Gail Blanke and Kathleen Walas, is based on the authors' professional experience with Avon Products' Women of Enterprise Awards, given each year to outstanding women entrepreneurs. The authors offer a specific plan to help you gain control over your life and include business tips and quizzes as well as beauty and lifestyle information. ($17.95 cloth)

SIDE-BY-SIDE STRATEGIES: *How Two-Career Couples Can Thrive in the Nineties,* by Jane Hershey Cuozzo and S. Diane Graham, describes how two-career couples can learn the difference between competing with a spouse and becoming a supportive Power Partner. Published in hardcover as *Power Partners.* ($10.95 paper, $19.95 cloth)

DARE TO CONFRONT: *How to Intervene When Someone You Care About Has an Alcohol or Drug Problem,* by Bob Wright and Deborah George Wright, shows the reader how to use the step-by-step methods of professional interventionists to motivate drug-dependent people to accept the help they need. ($17.95 cloth)

WORK WITH ME! *How to Make the Most of Office Support Staff,* by Betsy Lazary, shows how to find, train and nurture the "perfect" assistant and how best to utilize your support staff professionals. ($9.95 paper)

MANN FOR ALL SEASONS: *Wit and Wisdom from* The Washington Post*'s Judy Mann,* by Judy Mann, shows the columnist at her best as she writes about women, families and the politics of the women's revolution. ($9.95 paper, $19.95 cloth)

THE SOLUTION TO POLLUTION IN THE WORKPLACE, by Laurence Sombke, Terry M. Robertson and Elliot M. Kaplan, supplies employees with everything they need to know about cleaning up their workspace, including recycling, using energy efficiently, conserving water, buying recycled products and nontoxic supplies. ($9.95 paper)

THE ENVIRONMENTAL GARDENER: *The Solution to Pollution for Lawns and Gardens,* by Laurence Sombke, focuses on what each of us can do to protect our endangered plant life. A practical sourcebook and shopping guide. ($8.95 paper)

THE LOYALTY FACTOR: *Building Trust in Today's Workplace,* by Carol Kinsey Goman, Ph.D., offers techniques for restoring commitment and loyalty in the workplace. ($9.95 paper)

DARE TO CHANGE YOUR JOB—AND YOUR LIFE, by Carole Kanchier, Ph.D., provides a look at career growth and development throughout the life cycle. ($10.95 paper)

MISS AMERICA: *In Pursuit of the Crown,* by Ann-Marie Bivans, is an authorized guidebook to the Pageant, containing eyewitness accounts, complete historical data, and a realistic look at the trials and triumphs of potential Miss Americas. ($27.50 cloth)

POSITIVELY OUTRAGEOUS SERVICE: *New and Easy Ways to Win Customers for Life,* by T. Scott Gross, identifies what the consumers of the nineties really want and how businesses can develop effective marketing strategies to answer those needs. ($14.95 paper)

BREATHING SPACE: *Living and Working at a Comfortable Pace in a Sped-Up Society,* by Jeff Davidson, helps readers to handle information and activity overload and gain greater control over their lives ($10.95 paper)

TWENTYSOMETHING: *Managing and Motivating Today's New Work Force,* by Lawrence J. Bradford, Ph.D., and Claire Raines, M.A., examines the work orientation of the younger generation, offering managers in businesses of all kinds a practical guide to better understand and supervise their young employees. ($22.95 cloth)

BALANCING ACTS! *Juggling Love, Work, Family and Recreation,* by Susan Schiffer Stautberg and Marcia L. Worthing, provides strategies to achieve a balanced life by reordering priorities and setting realistic goals. ($12.95 paper)

THE OUTDOOR WOMAN: *A Handbook to Adventure,* by Patricia Hubbard and Stan Wass, details the lives of adventurous outdoor women and offers their ideas on how you can incorporate exciting outdoor experiences into your life. ($14.95 paper)

THE LIVING HEART: *Brand Name Shopper's Guide,* by Michael E. De-Bakey, M.D., Antonio M. Gotto, Jr., M.D., D.Phil., Lynne W. Scott, M.A., R.D./L.D., and John P. Foreyt, Ph.D., lists brand name supermarket products that are low in fat, saturated fatty acids, and cholesterol. ($12.95 paper)

MIND YOUR OWN BUSINESS: *And Keep It in the Family,* by Marcy Syms. Inside story of a family business told by the president and COO of Syms Corp. Interviews with members of forty other family-owned businesses. ($18.95 cloth)

REAL BEAUTY . . . REAL WOMEN: *A Workbook for Making the Best of Your Own Good Looks,* by Kathleen Walas, National Beauty and Fashion Director of Avon Products, offers expert advice on beauty and fashion to women of all ages and ethnic backgrounds. ($14.95 workbook)

MANAGING YOUR CHILD'S DIABETES, by Robert Wood Johnson IV, Sale Johnson, Casey Johnson, and Susan Kleinman, brings help to families trying to understand diabetes and control its effects. ($10.95 paper, $18.95 cloth)

A TEEN'S GUIDE TO ENTERPRISE: *Secrets of Business Success,* by Gail Blanke Cusick and Kate Cusick, provides guidance for teenagers who want to start their own businesses. ($7.95 paper)

STEP FORWARD: *Sexual Harassment in the Workplace, What You Need to Know,* by Susan L. Webb, teaches the reader the basic facts about sexual harassment, as well as furnishing procedures to help stop it. ($9.95 paper)